# — THE —
# REAL
# YOU

## Becoming *the* Person
## You Want *to* Be

# Dr. Kevin Leman

Fleming H. Revell
A Division of Baker Book House Co
Grand Rapids, Michigan 49516

Published by Fleming H. Revell
a division of Baker Book House Company
P.O. Box 6287, Grand Rapids, MI 49516-6287
www.bakerbooks.com

Paperback edition published 2003

Printed in the United States of America

The Library of Congress has cataloged the hardcover edition as follows:

Leman, Kevin.
    The real you : become the person you were meant to be /
Kevin Leman.
         p.    cm.
    Includes bibliographical references.
    ISBN 0-8007-1818-6
    1. Self-actualization (Psychology) 2. Typology 3. Birth order. I. Title.
BF637 .S4 L44 2002
158.1—dc21                           2002004085

ISBN 0-8007-5812-9 ( pbk.)
ISBN 0-8007-5864-1 (intl. pbk.)

# Contents

# I

## The Personality Makeover

When you think about it, this very second you are doing something absolutely amazing, almost mind-boggling. You're reading a book by Dr. Kevin Leman. Either you've checked it out of the library (you cheapskate!), borrowed it from a friend, received it as a gift, or plunked down your own hard-earned cash to figure out what I have to say.

What's so extraordinary about that?

Let me tell you.

I was one of those kids who was going no place in life—and taking his time to get there. If it weren't for three other even more hapless bottom dwellers than myself, I would have graduated dead last in my high school class. Everyone, including me, pretty much figured that Kevin

Leman would spend his entire career fixing flats and changing tires at the local gas station, selling newspapers at a street corner kiosk, or maybe even picking up the trash alongside the road.

To be honest with you, I thought I was dumber than mud.

Then one almost magical day in April of 1961 I had a conversation with a gray-haired math teacher that changed my life. She was a rather large old woman, somewhere between estrogen and death, her gray hair just on the verge of turning blue. She had seen literally thousands of students come and go through her school, including my perfect sister, Sally, and my "Mr. Most Likely to Succeed" brother, Jack, and she cornered me after one of my many incidents.

You see, I was a seventeen-year-old master of classroom incidents. One of my favorites was doing obscene wild birdcalls in class. I could get away with talking like a sailor because I did it like I was imitating a bird, and you had to listen carefully to hear that I was actually saying something dirty or making fun of the teacher. The teacher, of course, was usually trying to ignore me, leaving her no time to interpret my calls, so I had a field day making some of the students around me grab their sides in laughter.

If verbal humor didn't put me in the spotlight, I tried being a master performance artist—like the time during history class when I successfully crawled out of class on my hands and knees. It was a tremendous piece of work, if I may say so myself.

"Why would you *do* that?" some of you might be asking, and that's a fair question. The fact is, I didn't escape in order to get a drink of water, sneak into the boy's room to smoke, or get a candy bar at the store. In fact, I didn't even particularly want to leave the class—that was my audience, after all. I just craved attention and would do almost anything for a laugh, and I had raised the bar so high that to keep getting attention I had to do something really bizarre.

6

So this old teacher finally cornered me just a few months before graduation and said, "Kevin, I know you and I know your family. I've watched you over the years."

*Here it comes,* I thought. *Another lecture asking me why I can't be more like my brother and sister.*

But Miss Wilson went in an entirely different direction. "You know, it occurred to me the other day, and I wonder if it ever occurred to you, that maybe you could use some of the energy you expend on these antics you use around the school to really make something of yourself rather than just be the proverbial class clown—at your expense, I would add."

What shocked me about this conversation was that Miss Gray Hair saw something good in me. She saw this jerky little show-off kid, the baby of the family, putting on another embarrassing performance, but instead of seeing a loser, she saw potential. She had enough insight to challenge me by suggesting that I might be able to actually do something with my life; I didn't have to be a slave to the worst tendencies of my personality.

As I look back on my life and count the people who have really mattered, Miss Wilson is in the top five. If it hadn't been for her, you might have been reading *about* me (in the police blotter section of your newspaper), but you probably wouldn't be picking up a book written *by* me.

The psychologist in me wants to ask, "Now what made Kevin Leman so eager to grab attention when he was young?" As an adult, that's not a difficult question to answer: I had nowhere else to go.

## Where Else Could I Go?

Have you ever been around a Sally? Not your everyday Sally; not your youngest child Sally or a middle-born child named Sally. I'm talking about a first-born, every-hair-in-place, ever-competent, always trustwor-thy, and thoroughly dependable Sally.

Sally was my perfect sister, who, as a student, always told her girlfriends, "I think I really blew the test," then found out she got "only" 97 percent on it. Eight years older than me, Sally was in many ways like a second mother. I saw no flaws in her. If Jesus hadn't been born yet, I think she could have been a pretty good candidate for Mary's role. That's how highly I esteemed her.

My brother, Jack—who I not so affectionately referred to as "God"—was to guys what Sally was to girls. He cor-nered the market on success: quarterback of the football team, a strong student, handsome and popular, never wanting for women, very well liked, all the confidence of the oldest son.

Where was I supposed to go? I couldn't be a better stu-dent than Sally. I didn't have Jack's athletic prowess. Com-pared to him, I always felt scrawny (of course, he was older than me, but you don't think like that when you're a kid). There was no room for me to try to get noticed by being an excellent student or class leader. If I wanted attention, I'd have to look elsewhere, because Sally and Jack had cov-ered all the positive bases.

From behind my biased eyes, there was no other way to gain notoriety than by being a cutup. I was never really a mean-spirited kid; rather, I was looking to make people laugh. If it put me on center stage, so much the better.

My love of laughter came almost by accident. I was in second grade, seven years old, when Sally recruited me to be the mascot on her cheerleading squad. One time, in the middle of a game, I totally messed up a cheer. Initially I was embarrassed, but when I looked up into that sea of faces, watching everybody point at me and laugh, I remember thinking, *Hey, this isn't so bad,* and even milking it a little bit. This wasn't conscious; I was too young for that. But the desire to make a mark, to be noticed, to become someone is ingrained in us, and I had found my niche: I would spend my life making people laugh.

My gray-haired math teacher had watched all this with detached reserve. She recognized me as a people person; she saw how I manipulated my mother (who seemingly spent more time in school than I did) and realized that those powers of persuasion could be put to nobler uses.

It's not that I hadn't been lectured before, but all my teachers had said the same thing: "If Kevin would just apply himself, he could do so much better." My answer was always, why apply myself with hard work when I could have so much fun entertaining everybody? The fact that the teachers didn't like me didn't bother me one bit; most of the kids loved having me in their class. They pointed to each other as soon as they realized I'd be in their homeroom, whispering, "Oh, good! We've got Leman! This is gonna be a fun year!"

At first it almost bothered me that this old biddy could see through me, but something in her eyes told me she saw something that nobody else did and that I ought to give her a chance. She was a great teacher and ended up tutoring me my senior year, from April through June. "If you work a little harder, you still might graduate," she assured me.

So work I did—for perhaps the first time in my life. No one was more amazed by this than me. I just couldn't believe that I really felt like pleasing a teacher. I had never done that before—it was an entirely new experience, and it paid off. I flunked just one class that semester—a record for me. (Whereas my mom expected all A's and an occasional B from my brother and sister, she got on her knees to pray that I could pull out the occasional C, just to reassure herself that, in her words, "God didn't forget to put a brain in that boy.")

I'll never forget the afternoon I walked up to the posted list at school that carried the names of all the seniors who would be graduating the next day. There was my name, bigger than life. Now *I* was the one laughing. I said to myself, *Well, Leman, you did it. You're going to be a high school graduate. You may never accomplish anything else in your life, but this is something you got done.*

## Getting Better

It's a long story that I've told elsewhere, but after a little ingenuity, I actually convinced a college to accept me. Not only did I get into college, but I continually surprised myself: I started to succeed, albeit at my own level. While this might surprise those of you who are bona fide Goody Two-shoes, the other cutups will empathize when I admit that this new successful Kevin Leman was not a Kevin Leman I was comfortable with. I had never seen myself as successful, and it took me some time to adjust my perceptions. I'll never forget looking at that first college report card: I saw all C's and just one D. While such a report card would have horrified my sister, Sally, it made me feel tremendous. I remember thinking, *I'm in college; those are C's, which means for the most part I am doing average college work—that's pretty good.*

The second trimester, I did about the same, except that I got an A in baseball. Unfortunately, during my third trimester I ran into kinesiology (or better said, kinesiology ran into me). At that point in my life, I was thinking of maybe becoming a P.E. teacher. I loved sports and thought, *If they want to pay me for being in charge of seven hours of recreation, that's not a bad gig.*

Unfortunately, the old Kevin kept resurrecting himself, and the school threw me out for a little prank that a dean took a little too seriously. Out of options, I went home to my parents in Tucson, Arizona.

Picture this: I was nineteen years old, thrown out of college, with not much hope for the future. I got a job as a janitor in a medical center, which probably in some way reflected what I thought about myself. I worked there for about five years, during which time I met my wife, Sande, who watered the seeds sown by my high school math teacher. Sande is the person who is probably most responsible for the fact that you are holding a book written by me in your hands.

With Sande's inspiration, I went back to college, this time the University of Arizona, and proceeded to flunk the same course twice, but there was something about Sande that made me want to do better, to not give in to my darker side. When I finally got into the university full time, I was practically dumbfounded by my first report card: all A's except for one B, which qualified me for the dean's list.

I remember reading my name out loud: "Kevin Leman, on the dean's list," feeling a sense of pride for the grades I earned, but also struggling with a sense of disbelief. The grades were totally inconsistent with how I saw myself, but I did it again the next semester. After that, I received a notice in the mail from the university, telling me that I had received University Scholarship Honors. I thought, *They're actually going to pay me to finish college!* I was poor, so the money really helped.

The next few years only widened the gap between my perceptions of my real self and my ideal self. I became a member of *Psy Chi,* a national honor society for psychology students, shocked myself even further by getting into a master's program with relative ease, and then even went on to get a doctorate degree.

As I would have said as a high school student, "Who would have ever thunk it?"

So you're reading a book written by a guy who was going nowhere but who somehow ended up getting at least a few things done. But why a book on personality? And what does my past have to do with this subject?

## What You Want

Let me make some hunches about why you've picked up this book. I doubt that too many of you saw my picture on the back and thought, *Wow! What an amazing guy! I bet he has a lot to say!* Instead, you were stopped short by the title. You're interested in finding out more about what makes you the way you are. Maybe you've always wondered why you're so very different from your siblings—after all, you grew up in the same home environment and had the same parents, but you probably represent opposite points on the personality scale.

Why is that?

In short, you want to know what kind of personality you have—is it a "good" personality, a winning personality, a destructive personality?

But the mere fact that you're asking that question shows me that you have another aim in mind—you're wondering if you might be able to use this book to *improve* your personality. Maybe you wish you could be more outgoing, more sociable, or more confident. Maybe you've been told you have a grating personality and you want a completely different you. You're sort of like the women who come on *Oprah* for those makeover changes—straight hair, drab clothing, and poorly applied makeup, crying out, "I need a change. What I've got just isn't working!" Forty minutes later these same women walk out looking like models—or at least like attractive anchorwomen.

Well, it'll take us more than forty minutes, but I believe personality makeovers are just as possible as appearance makeovers. I've seen it happen too many times to believe otherwise.

The first step toward changing your personality or behavior is to take a look at your personality and decide what it is you want to change (I want to be more extroverted, have more friends; I'm too dull, too boring, etc.). Most of us are operating in personality ruts that have been forged over the years, and getting out of a rut isn't easy—just ask Bryant Gumbel.

In 1999, after fifteen years of working on the *Today* show at NBC, Bryant started hosting CBS's new *The Early Show*. For fifteen years, Bryant made countless transitions into commercials by saying, "This is *Today* on NBC." Now he was on a new show with a new network.

Old habits die hard. During his first week on the air, the inevitable happened. While on the CBS *Early Show*, Bryant fell back into old patterns and welcomed his viewers by saying, "This is *Today* on NBC."

There was an awkward silence, a little laughter, and the show carried on. Steve Friedman, the producer, was sympathetic toward Bryant's miscue. "You say something four or five times a day for 15 years, and it's kind of hard to break. I figure Bryant said it 15,000 times at *Today;* now make it 15,001."[1]

All of us have these same ruts. We may not be on camera, but we've conditioned ourselves to say and do things and to respond in certain ways that have become second nature to us. We don't even think about them.

Well, in this book I'm going to do my best to get you to rethink everything you've been doing, all the assumptions you hold, and even the rule book you live by. No, you may never have realized that you even have a rule book, but let me assure you that you do. It's there, and for some of you, it's ruining your life!

I don't want to make you into an entirely different person—in many ways I'll always be the class clown—because it's important for you to build on your natural strengths rather than try to create an artificial personality. But I do want to help you stop destructive behavior as well as learn how to maximize the latent strengths you may not even realize lie hidden within your soul. Helping people in this way has become something of a personal mission of mine—in large part because of my own experience.

## Are You Less than You Were Meant to Be?

I wasted so many years by selling myself short, by not believing in myself, by always saying, "My brother or sister could do that, but I can't."

Have you ever been there? Have you ever felt that you could be so much more—not just in your vocation but in your relationships and among your circle of friends—but you keep falling back into old destructive patterns?

I wish I could give you five easy steps to set your life back on track. Unfortunately, I can't. As you've already seen, my own recovery was a long process with a lot of work and many setbacks. It took me years—literally *years*—to learn how to think differently of myself.

While I can't offer a quick fix, I can offer hope. After all, you're holding my twenty-second book in your hands; thirty years ago, who would have ever believed Kevin Leman could *read* twenty-two books, much less write them! Leman books have killed a forest full of trees—they are printed in thirteen different languages. My seminars have been attended by tens of thousands, and I've spoken to hundreds of millions on radio and television. I don't say this boastfully, but with utter astonishment. Knowing my weaknesses as well as I do, not to mention my early childhood capers, it is astonishing to me what is happening today.

That brings us back to you. Once you really understand yourself—your strengths and weaknesses, your predispositions, your family background, and the forces of nature that have shaped you into the person you are—there will be no holding you back. You can climb vocational mountains, break out of relational ruts, and forge new social patterns. This is your invitation to become someone you've always wanted to be, but perhaps you've never known how to get there. I know what I'm talking about here. I fought success. I didn't see myself as anything but a failure. But life has worked out mighty fine for me, and it can for you as well.

## The Road Map to Your Personality

We're going to begin our exploration of what makes you you by discussing the four basic temperaments. These are traditional labels that help people get a grip on the personality traits that distinguish them from someone else. Some people think they're born melancholy or choleric, sanguine or phlegmatic (don't worry—I'll explain what each of those mean in a later chapter)—but have you ever noticed that every family seems to be a rather diverse bunch? You almost never see a family full of melancholies, for instance. Why is that?

Next, we'll talk about the powerful shaping influence of birth order. A good bit of your life script was written for you based on decisions made by your parents—how many kids they would have, what order they had them in, etc. You can't fully understand yourself without understanding the family dynamics in which you were raised.

In the third section, we'll turn our attention to early childhood memories. While the four temperaments describe who you are, and birth order helps to explain how you got there, early childhood memories reveal your unspoken assumptions about life. They provide a key to unlock the mystery of why you see things the way you do, why certain things bug you that don't bug others, and why some things comfort you that frighten others.

In section four, we'll take the knowledge gained from the first three sections and explore your love language.

15

You are not an autonomous individual but a person who is involved in many relationships. Understanding your love language will help you gain a better understanding of how to succeed in these interpersonal connections.

Finally, we'll put all four personality indicators together and help you do a self-evaluation, revealing your strengths and weaknesses, your biases, your basic assumptions about life, and your map for relational success. My promise to you is this: If you read this entire book, after you put it down you're going to know why you are the way you are and also have a good idea about how to improve those areas that have held you back.

The good news is you don't have to be mired in a non-productive or even self-destructive lifestyle—you can become a different person. To do that, you need to gain a better self-awareness, and you've got to begin to think differently.

Sound interesting? Then let's get started!

# PART 1

# THE
# FOUR
# PERSONALITIES

# 2

# Many People, Four Flavors

As the father of five children, I've spent more than my share of time reading children's stories and watching the occasional children's program. One of my favorites has always been A. A. Milne's classic, *Winnie the Pooh*.

What makes Milne's work so great is that it rings true to life. Each character has a distinct personality: There's the fun-loving Tigger, always eager to bounce around, have a good time, and enjoy the day. There's the hyper, uptight Rabbit, obsessed with perfection, wanting everything—from the planting of his vegetable garden to arriving on time—done just right. There's the lovable Winnie the Pooh, the peacemaker, who sees the good in everybody and just wishes that everybody would get along. And there's the paternal Christopher Robin, who puts up with these characters but always comes off as being the one who is right—even though he is just a young boy himself.

Some of you may have realized that in the characters of Pooh, I've just described the four basic personality temperaments: popular sanguines, powerful cholerics, perfect melancholies, and peaceful phlegmatics.[1] These four temperaments were first mentioned by Hippocrates over two thousand years ago, hundreds of years before Christ was born. Through the ages, they have served as reliable descriptors of basic personality types.

Today's recognized authority on the four temperaments is Florence Littauer, whose book *Personality Plus* has introduced a generation to this teaching. I know Florence, and many years ago we agreed that I'd talk on birth order and she'd talk on the temperaments; so much of what I say is based on work she and her husband, Fred, have done. If you really want to get into this temperament stuff—and I'd encourage you to do so—pick up a copy of her best-seller, *Personality Plus*.

Personality typing can't explain *how* you became the person you are, but it is very helpful to describe you as you've become. Because of this, the temperaments make an excellent beginning point for our journey into the wonderful person you are. Let's look at each personality type in turn.

## Sanguines

Sanguines—the "Tiggers"—are often called "popular" because they're the social bunch, the kind you like to have show up at every party. Their motto is "Let's do it the fun way." Sanguines' needs are mostly social; that is, they want to be noticed, appreciated, affirmed, accepted, even adored.

Sanguines aren't difficult to identify: Search for the person who can talk about anything at any time in any situation, listen for the loudest person in the group, and watch out for the person with the biggest smile. Sanguines are usually most comfortable in a crowd, or at least in a small group. They have a bubbly personality, an almost naïve optimism, a strong sense of humor, and the innate ability to tell good stories. Most of all, they enjoy people and social interaction. They tend to be animated and playful, spontaneous and optimistic, funny and lively.

Sanguines also have weaknesses. They are so disorganized that they spend half their life looking for their car keys and the other half apologizing for missed appointments. They can't remember your name (but will be very offended if you forget theirs), have a tendency to exaggerate, and aren't particularly serious. Their "What? Me worry?" attitude means they are more than willing to let others do the work, and their eternal optimism makes them prime targets to be deceived.

What gets sanguines down? Boredom is a big one. They don't have much tolerance for that. Rejection is another. They live for approval and honestly can't believe that somebody doesn't find them just *adorable*. Sanguines are practically allergic to budgeting either their time or money—they get there when they get there, and if they want something they'll probably buy it regardless of how much debt they carry.

If you want to make a sanguine like you, it's pretty easy: Show an active interest in them, laugh at their jokes, and point out their positive characteristics. Do these things and you'll have a friend for life. Treat them well, and sanguines will inspire others, motivate others, and entertain others—just don't expect them to follow through or pay attention to detail.

If you want to ruin a sanguine's day, don't laugh at their jokes. Instead, criticize them or say something like, "Not everyone thinks you're cute." You'll see their face fall past China.

When under stress, sanguines tend to leave the scene, go shopping, and find someone who approves of them. If they can't do that, they'll blame others or create some excuse, however lame.

I have a particular affinity for sanguines. They're my favorites, in fact. Just my saying that should have clued you in to the fact that I am, of course, a sanguine myself. How does this play itself out? Let me show you.

Back in the mid-eighties, money was a little tight for the Leman household. I hadn't sold quite as many books, wasn't doing quite as many seminars, and was still just finding my way in the world. I was walking through a shopping mall one day, just running in to get some socks or underwear or something mundane like that, when I walked by a jewelry store. I got a glimpse of something, just out of the corner of my eye, that stopped me short. It was so amazing that I did a double take, walked backward, and practically twisted my neck off just to get a second look.

*Shazam!* I said to myself. There, under the high intensity of a showpiece lamp, sparkled the most amazing timepiece I had ever seen. It was just incredible. Calling this thing a watch is an understatement. It was practically the key to contentment, at least in my opinion. Its forty-eight diamonds around the face screamed, "I belong to somebody important!"

Immediately I started talking to myself. *I've never seen a watch like that in my entire life.*

The clerk saw her mark and quickly walked up, asking me if I'd like to hold it.

"Is that legal?" I asked.

She laughed and said, "Here, let's put it on you."

"Gosh, that's heavy," I said. "Is it gold?"

"Absolutely. It's 24-karat."

Before I could ask, "How much?" she said, "And it's on sale."

Shazam! It's on sale! Regularly $4,995, it was now going for a mere $3,800. Without thinking that the watch represented four months' income, I whipped out my American Express card and took the watch home.

It may shock some of you when I mention that, initially, I had absolutely no remorse. On the contrary, at the stoplights I couldn't stop stroking my ear with my left hand, letting everyone see just how important I was—the watch proved it! Light jumped off that sucker like crickets off summertime grass.

About a mile from home, however, reality finally accosted me. Mrs. Choleric—my wife—would be waiting for me.

I walked in the door and Sande took one look at my arm and said, "You bought that?"

"Yeah. Isn't it great?"

"That's the tackiest watch I've ever seen! How much did it cost?"

"It was sort of expensive, but I like it."

Are you getting the sanguine personality? Back then I knew we didn't have anywhere near $3,800 to spend on a watch, especially when I could have purchased a workable one for 1 percent of that amount. It didn't make me feel guilty to whip out the credit card. I saw something, I wanted it, and I bought it.

That's the sanguine way: Do something spontaneous, jump in with both feet, and ask questions later.

Now get this: Three days later, the dumb four-thousand dollar watch stopped working! I went back to the store, and the lady who sold it wasn't there. I was more than a little put out. You pay $3,800 for a watch, you expect it to last more than seventy-two hours, right?

"Hey," I told the new guy behind the counter, "my watch stopped, and it's only three days old!"

"Let me take a look at it," he said. "Oh, I see the problem."

"What's that?"

"You didn't wind it."

"You mean I have to wind this stupid watch?"

"Yes, sir."

A daily task—even one as small as winding a watch—is often more than a sanguine can handle.

I still have the watch and wear it everywhere I go. Ask me to show it to you if you come to one of my seminars. Though I now agree with Sande that it's a bit gaudy, it serves as my reminder about how easy it is to get hung up on things. A choleric would save the watch for very special occasions. Dr. Leman the sanguine wears it all the time, and it shows. It's a diamond shy by now, with a few nicks.

I've learned as I've grown older that flashy isn't good. Sande, my lovely choleric, has helped me in that respect, but I still carry marks of being a sanguine. I can't tell you how many times I've bought a used car without even starting it. If it looked right, it was mine. That's the sanguine way.

## Powerful Cholerics

Cholerics eat, sleep, and drink power and control. Whereas sanguines say, "Let's do it the fun way," the choleric's mantra is "Let's do it *my* way." Cholerics' favorite emotional menu is obedience (toward them), appreciation for accomplishments, and respect for their ability. If you serve these dishes on a daily basis, you'll have a strong ally. If you withhold them, you'll have a fierce adversary.

Cholerics come in handy when you need someone to take charge and make snappy (usually correct) judgments. Their self-confidence is high, and never once in their life have they feared hurting other people's feelings, so they tend to be decisive, firm, and commanding. You couldn't ask for a better military commander or football coach. They are adventurous, persuasive, strong-willed, competitive, outspoken, daring, confident, and independent.

On the negative side, cholerics can become a bit bossy, domineering, insensitive, and impatient. They expect immediate and enthusiastic compliance and can take it personally if their judgment is even questioned. While they don't appear to have any fears, if you scratch the surface a few inches, you'll soon discover a strong fear of losing control; even the thought of mutiny could make them break out in a drenching sweat. Missing out on a promotion (or worse, being fired from a job), facing a serious illness, raising a rebellious child—these are the nightmare scenarios for control-oriented cholerics. They also tend to be unsympathetic, unaffectionate, headstrong, proud, intolerant, short-tempered, and overly dedicated to work.

They get along best with submissive and supportive people pleasers who see things their way and when asked to jump quickly respond, "How high?" If you really want to get on a choleric's good side, let them get the credit for something you've done. Cooperate with their suggestions and work hard to make them look good.

The reverse will soon make a choleric a bitter enemy: Steal their limelight, act like a rebellious troublemaker, question their judgment, sidestep their authority, act independently, and just watch the steam come out of their ears!

Cholerics keep the world moving and improving. They are right most of the time and can accomplish more in ten years than most sanguines will get done in a lifetime. They'd do even better if they could learn to delegate more and became a little more patient, but true cholerics will have to learn how to be more sensitive and less controlling—it certainly won't come naturally.

Cholerics respond to stress by outworking the problem. They become even more controlling and put in more hours, convinced they can solve any problem they face with just a bit more effort. Their tolerance level is such that they shed few tears getting rid of a troublesome employee.

Remember, if you're hunting for a choleric, look for someone who has supreme self-confidence, likes to be in control, and is comfortable making quick decisions.

## Melancholies

I'm not much when it comes to tools. In fact, I'm awful when it comes to tools, so you can imagine my dismay when, after purchasing an "easy to assemble" dollhouse for one of the girls, about 1,385,432 parts fell out of the box. Sande's eyes went wide—any more than five parts and I'm out of my league—and she said what I was thinking: "Better pay Roger a visit."

Roger is a perfect melancholy. Whereas the sanguine says, "Let's do it the fun way," and the choleric says, "Let's do it my way," the melancholy says, "Let's do it the right way."

I can't tell you how many times Roger stopped me when I was just about to do something and said, "Now, if we really want to do this right . . ."

Melancholies put a lot of emotional energy into getting something done correctly. They have a strong emotional attachment to stability, and their need to get something right often translates into a need for space, silence, and sensitivity. While the cholerics get things done, the melancholies think about how it *should* be done. They're the philosophers among us who enjoy deep analysis, live by high standards and ideals, are skilled at setting long-range goals, and tend to be very organized. In addition to being highly analytical, melancholies are usually respectful, sensitive, good planners, orderly, faithful, cultured, idealistic, thoughtful, and loyal—not a bad combination.

Their weaknesses? Think anal retentive! That's right— they spend too much time on preparation and too much time worrying about messing things up. Their near obsession with details and the process means they can become easily depressed, weighted down by negatives, and often suspicious of others.

If their high standards aren't met—or just as hurtful, no one seems to care about them—it's hard for a melancholy to even get out of bed. They may have nightmares about making a mistake and take it personally and deeply if they believe they are forced to compromise their standards or to lower their ideals. They are insecure to begin with and tend to be rather unforgiving and resentful. Furthermore, their highly analytical nature makes them hard to please, pessimistic, negatively bent, moody, and skeptical; they are often loners. They are suspicious and when crossed can become out-and-out revengeful.

Melancholies love to hang out with the serious crowd; they look for people who enjoy deep discussions and have little patience for clown personalities. If someone is considered an intellectual lightweight or is disorganized, superficial, or even just plain old unpredictable, melancholies run in the other direction—or marry them. They're famous for choosing a popular sanguine spouse, hoping to piggyback on the sanguine's social skills, then turning around and immediately trying to place their sanguine on a disciplined schedule.

Fat chance!

Melancholies can be brooding and very sensitive, but they are also usually marked by good manners, self-deprecation, and obvious attention to detail—including in their grooming.

## Phlegmatics

"Can't we all just get along?" That's the song of the phlegmatic, who suggests, "Let's do it the easy way."

Phlegmatics avoid conflict like toddlers run from bedtime. They devote a generous portion of their life to keeping the peace and sidestepping conflicts, though they are usually pretty good at objectively solving problems. They tend to have a balanced and pleasing personality as well as an even disposition (they're always "just fine") and are wonderfully adaptable, patient, obliging, and friendly, not to mention good at listening (you couldn't have a better neighbor). They run on the submissive side and seem to have the gift of being contented. Phlegmatics are usually tolerant and diplomatic and go out of their way to be inoffensive.

Phlegmatics' weaknesses result from their quiet side: a lack of enthusiasm and energy, and sometimes a chronic inability to make a decision. They don't want to disappoint anybody. While they are a calming influence to those around them—phlegmatics are the type who never get too easily excited, even in the midst of crisis—it wouldn't hurt them to become a little more self-motivated and a little better at setting goals. Their indecisiveness can become irritating, and some take a decided bent toward being a worrier. Their mumbling speech and sluggish approach to life can border on laziness and aimlessness.

As calm, cool, and collected individuals, phlegmatics aren't likely to make impulsive decisions. They are often popular because they are rarely offensive. They have a keen sense of propriety and seek to fit right in. Don't expect a phlegmatic to flake out. They'll hang in there until the last dog is hung.

## Have Wallpaper, Will Murder

One of the most dramatic examples I've ever witnessed regarding the different temperaments took place nearly three decades ago when my wife agreed to wallpaper my mom's kitchen. Two of my dad's friends showed up, both of whom happened to be retired colonels in the Air Force. One of them was an obvious melancholy, the other a choleric. Being military men, they decided to take action and help my wife with the wallpapering. I have to admit, the sanguine in me laughed and thought, "This could get fun."

You have to understand, I married Martha Stewart's clone. If Martha ever took a vacation, Sande could step right into her place and probably increase Martha's television ratings to boot. The last thing Sande needed while wallpapering that kitchen was advice—but she was about to get plenty.

As suggestion followed suggestion, I could see Sande's temperature begin to rise. The melancholic colonel wanted this job done right. The choleric was adamant that it be done his way, and it took the two men all of ten seconds to start raising their voices at each other.

"Now, Sande," the melancholy offered, "make sure you get that plumb line straight. Otherwise the entire job will be messed up."

"You sound like you know what you're talking about," I offered. "Have you wallpapered much before?"

"He couldn't wallpaper a doghouse," the choleric cut in. "He hasn't papered a square inch!"

"Neither have you!" the melancholy said in his defense.

This was too rich—neither of them had any experience wallpapering, yet both of them felt that Sande couldn't possibly do the job without their help.

Not even close to being deterred, the melancholy weighed in with his preferred method. "The best way to do this is to put a weight on the bottom of your string there," he said. "Once the string is taut, you've got your plumb line."

"Could you be any more dense?" the choleric challenged him. "If she just leaves the line there, it'll move every time she touches it! She should chalk the line, snap it against the wall, and she won't have to worry about working around it."

I'm not sure how many plumb lines Sande has prepared—I'm guessing more than a dozen, not one of which took her more than five minutes. But thanks to these two guys, it took Sande a good hour and a half just to get a plumb line on the wall.

Everything became a battle between doing it the "right way" and doing it "my way." Both colonels had very strong opinions about where Sande should start to hang the paper; both were even more forceful about how to cut a corner, how to paper over switches, and the best way to line up the paper against the ceiling. And when Sande reached an air conditioning duct—my goodness, you would have thought the future of democracy was on the line by the way these men argued their cases.

I couldn't help but chuckle when my mother, the classic phlegmatic, entered the scene. She was clearly uncomfortable with all the arguing, and as a phlegmatic, she was sure it was all her fault—after all, it was her kitchen that everyone was arguing over—so she went back to her old standby. In my mother's worldview, if there's a problem, you bake your way out of it.

"Can I get you gentlemen some cookies and coffee?" she offered.

She might just as well have landed on the beaches of Normandy during D day, offering tea and biscuits. They looked at her like she was from another planet. "Cookies? Coffee?" they seemed to be thinking. "Are you crazy? We've got a war going on here!"

Frankly, my mom should have stayed out of the kitchen. When she stayed, Mr. Melancholy and Colonel Choleric enlisted her in the war.

"What do you think of this corner, May?" Colonel Choleric asked.

"It looks fine," Mom said.

"*Fine?*" Mr. Melancholy nearly shouted. "You think this is *fine?* Look at this bulge here. See? See the problem?"

"Oh yeah," Mom said, totally unsuspecting, "you're right."

"Of course he's not right," Colonel Choleric cut in. He then spent five minutes making his case.

"Yes, yes, I see that now," Mom said, only to be accosted by Mr. Melancholy.

When Sande started to book the paper (rolling it, putting it in a tub of water, letting it soak, then unfolding it to put it on the wall), I just about died laughing. Booking is a complicated process that needs to be done rather quickly. Sande is competent, but she's not a perfectionist. She just wanted to get the paper up on the wall, whereas the two colonels had their own agendas and were trying to direct her every move. This slowed Sande down and made the job that much more difficult.

I have to confess, the sanguine in me couldn't stop from egging the two colonels on just a little bit. "You know, Ken, you ought to listen to him more," I said once. "He sounds like he knows what he's doing." Of course, I knew this would make Ken furious, and he'd plead his case all the more, but a sanguine's role is to make things fun.

Now consider this story as it relates to you. If you were in it, what role would you play? Would you be like me, goading people on and trying to have a good time? Would you be concerned with the correct way to hang the wallpaper? Would you be the powerful choleric, who wants it done your way? Or would you be like my mom, trying to keep the peace as people go to war?

Whenever you're trying to keep the temperaments straight, remember this story—Mr. Melancholy was determined to get things done *right*; Mr. Choleric was just as determined to get things done *his way*; my mom, Mrs. Phlegmatic, was insistent that everybody just get along; and I, Mr. Sanguine, wanted to have a really good time.

Eventually, the inevitable happened—the two colonels stopped just short of coming to blows, and one of them stomped out of the house in a huff. Sande breathed a sigh of well-deserved relief, until Mr. Melancholy broke in with the words, "Now that he's gone we can really get this done right!"

As a sanguine, I'm not going to be as uptight as Mr. Melancholy, but I think you've got the picture by now.

"This all makes great sense, Leman," some of you might be saying. "But what if I don't fit any one particular mold?"

It's time to look at temperament blends.

## You're a Unique Blend

Florence Littauer was a young bride on her honeymoon, casually enjoying some grapes on a beach in Bermuda, when her husband asked her, "Do you like grapes?"

"Oh, I love grapes!" Florence replied.

"Then I assume you'd like to know how to eat them correctly?" Fred asked.

Florence was confused. No one had ever told her there was a right and a wrong way to eat grapes. "What did I do wrong?" she asked.

"It's not that you're doing it *wrong*," her new husband replied. "You're just not doing it right."

Florence pulled her grapes one by one directly off the big bunch, which, in Fred's view, left the bunch a wreck. Fred suggested that Florence should cut off a small bunch and pick her grapes off that, leaving the bigger bunch intact and more attractive.

Florence still didn't get it. She recounts, "I glanced around the secluded patio to see if there were some hidden group of grape judges waiting to enter my bunch in a contest, but seeing none, I said, 'Who cares?'"[2]

What was going on? Florence is a classic sanguine; Fred, as you've probably guessed, is clearly a melancholy. As far as a melancholy is concerned, there is a right way and a wrong way to do everything—including eating grapes.

To make matters more explosive, both Florence and Fred are somewhat choleric; that is, both like to be in control. A phlegmatic would have taken Fred's advice and said, "Whatever you say, dear," but not a sanguine with choleric tendencies.

Fred and Florence's experience points out an important dynamic. As you read through the four temperaments, you may have been thinking, "That sounds like me, but that one sounds a little like me too." The fact is, only a very rare person is 100 percent choleric, 100 percent sanguine, 100 percent phlegmatic, or 100 percent melancholy. Most of us are unique blends.

This only makes sense, doesn't it? Obviously, there are more than four personalities in the entire world. Each person is unique, and that uniqueness comes from the blend of our temperaments as filtered through the personal experiences that shape us.

While it's easy to make blanket statements such as, "All sanguines are the same," "All melancholies are pessimistic," etc., the truth is usually far subtler than that. In the rest of this book, we'll explore some other ways to help us understand ourselves better.

In fact, we'll begin doing this in the very next chapter, addressing one of my favorite issues: birth order.

# PART 2

# BIRTH ORDER

### WHY YOU ARE
### THE WAY YOU ARE

# 3

# Understanding Your Place in the Family Zoo

During my author's tour for the book *Sex Begins in the Kitchen,* I was speaking on a national television program. The tour was fun for me, in part because the kitchen is one of my favorite rooms in the house, and sex is one of my favorite pastimes. Put those two together, and I'm a happy man.

In the middle of our discussion, I said something like, "You know, as the baby, it's very strange to me that my wife, the first born, thinks things ought to be written down—like checks. I'm content to let the bank tell me what I have every month rather than go through all that trouble to find a missing dime."

The host stopped me and said, "Wait a minute—you called yourself a baby and your wife a first born. What do you mean 'baby'?"

"I'm the youngest born in my family."

"You know, you *do* remind me of my little brother," the host said.

I could see that this conversation was going to take a sharp left-hand turn. It always does whenever birth order is mentioned. Instead of fighting it, I decided to have a little fun (very much a last-born trait, by the way). I noticed that the host had all of her little questions for the interview meticulously typed on two sheets of paper. I could see "Question number 1," "Question number 2," etc. She had built a ten-foot-high wall against any smidgen of spontaneity that might somehow sneak into her interview. No doubt in my mind, I was dealing with a first born.

*This oughta be fun,* I said to myself just before I leaned over, took the notes out of the host's hands, crumpled them up, and threw them over my left shoulder.

"You don't need those notes," I told her. "Let's just talk to each other."

The host was horrified. She put her hands to the sides of her face, took on the appearance of a woman who had seen a ghost, and then remembered she was on live TV!

The production people lost it. They were howling behind the camera. They had never seen the host put in this position before, and boy, were they enjoying it.

"Now you *really* remind me of my little brother," she said.

The first borns watching that interview were probably thinking, "That little brat! He needs a good spanking!"

The last borns were giving each other high fives and generally celebrating. (By the way, if any television hosts are reading this book and worried about having me on their show, I'd never do this to you—I promise!)

The host reminded me of my oldest (and only) sister, Sally. Sally can't believe I can get up in front of five or ten thousand people and talk for an hour without using a single note card. She's even more dumbfounded that I can be given the topic just an hour or so before I get up to talk. When Sally speaks, she wants to rehearse her talk forty-two times; and even after that she brings ten pages of notes with yellow highlights throughout.

In case you first borns are wondering, "Why did you pull those notes out of the host's hands?" let me give you an answer that may simply make you cringe. The truth is, I did it just to be a brat; it was my spontaneous side breaking out.

Sometimes this spontaneous side can get me in trouble. I have appeared on *Good Morning America* several times, but on one particular occasion they asked me to stay over and do another spot (something that is very rare). We were talking about Barbie dolls and the damage they can do by telling young girls they have to aspire after impossible body types, when I got a little too explicit in one description. I caught myself right afterward, then asked Charlie and Joan, on air, "Is it okay for me to say 'little boobies' on the air?"

Though I initially regretted my lapse, it was a familiar emotion. Regret is a last born's natural state—we usually speak first and thus get to be on a first-name basis with regret and the word "oops." I have to confess, however, that when I saw the production people doubled over with laughter after I asked, "Is it okay to say 'little boobies'?" I felt pretty good about the interview!

Throughout my professional life, I have found birth order to fascinate people. As a last born, I like to have fun with it. Just the other day, I met a pastor who was dressed immaculately, whose fingernails were so meticulously trimmed that his hands could be used in a magazine ad, and whose hairstyle looked like it belonged in a *GQ* spread.

"You're a first-born son, aren't you?" I asked him.

He looked at me like, *How can you know that? Why did you say that? Did someone tell you something?*

To me, it's fun just to see their wheels turning.

"Why do you say that?" he asked.

"You are, aren't you?"

"Yes, but how'd you know that?"

"Oh, just a guess . . ."

"No, really, someone must have told you, right? Someone's playing a trick on me."

"No, I haven't talked to anyone. But I'm a psychologist who has studied birth order."

It's a great icebreaker and a delightful form of self-entertainment. One of the most popular parts of my seminars occurs when I have people stand up and I begin telling them, with about 90 percent accuracy, their own birth order.

That's why, to be honest with you, I much prefer talking about birth order than about the four temperaments. Nobody would be surprised if I said, "I bet you're a melancholy." Some of them probably wouldn't even know what I was talking about. But when I guess the order in which someone was born into their family, that's when I really get a reaction.

Don't get me wrong—I believe the temperaments provide a helpful description of basic personality types. In fact, I bet that while many of you were reading through the temperaments, most of you were saying, "Yeah, that's me. I guess I was born that way; it's my genes." If that were true—that you were simply born that way because of your genetic code, doesn't it seem odd to you that families aren't usually made up of all melancholies, all cholerics, all sanguines, or all phlegmatics? Of course, if a phlegmatic marries a choleric, you might expect a mixture of the two, but how can you account for the fact that a large family will have all four temperaments represented?

My guess is that the sanguine *becomes* a sanguine because she realizes the one above her is anything but a sanguine.

The first born is a choleric because his parents raised him in such a way that he takes on choleric (first-born) tendencies. What you end up with is a branching-off effect where kids intuit what situation they are born into and learn to act accordingly to find their own place and role in the family.

While I don't mean to suggest that every first born will be choleric and every last born will be sanguine, what I am suggesting is that you'll find far more first-born cholerics than you'll find last-born cholerics. We are a product of the environment in which we grew up; while our genes create certain parameters and determine a lot about who we are and what we become, we are also greatly shaped by our experiences and the expressions we see on people's faces from the time we're babies.

While the temperaments describe who we are, birth order helps to explain why we've become that way. The theory behind birth order is this: The order in which we were born into our family shapes our personality in indelible ways. First borns generally share common characteristics, as do last borns and middle borns. Birth order also takes into account that children react to the kids above them, usually going in an opposite direction.

As a proponent of birth order, I believe that if you were to clone two women with the exact same DNA and place one of them as the baby of the family, with three older brothers, and place the other one as the oldest born, with three younger brothers, those two women would have markedly different personalities. They would still share some common characteristics, but the influence of birth order would largely prevail. The oldest sister, more likely than not, would be a great nurturer of men, while the younger sister would be a better friend to men—she'd understand them better and might even be more of a tomboy than a "mother." Their intelligence would be the

41

same, but how they used that intelligence and how they related to others would be remarkably different.

If you really want to understand your personality, including why you are the way you are, you're going to have to take a close look at your family of origin.

## The Launching Pad

Alfred Adler, the pioneer of birth-order theory, first developed the system that says most of us fall into four basic categories: first born, last born, middle born, and only born. Let's review some of the most marked characteristics of each birth order.

### The "Special" One

A friend of mine was talking to his eight-year-old daughter, the last born in his family, about a pack of Pez candy and a dispenser in a box of Cheerios. The middle-born son wanted the candy, the oldest daughter wanted the dispenser, and the youngest daughter wanted both.

"Why should I give you *both* the candy and the dispenser, while your brother and sister get nothing?" Dad asked his eight-year-old.

"Because I'm the youngest," she said.

Made plenty of sense to her!

Last borns grow up with a tremendous, unflagging sense of entitlement. You usually don't have to convince last borns that they are special—they already know it and will remind you every ten minutes should you ever momentarily forget. Because they are often coddled and babied—not just by Mom and Dad but also often by older siblings—last borns usually grow up to be "people persons." Since everyone in the family is older than they are, they have learned the art of persuasion and occasionally even manipulation. They can charm you, are usually engaging, and are often blatant show-offs. An overwhelming number of comedians are last borns.

A few years ago, I was asked to appear on the *Leeza Gibbons* show. The producers decided they wanted to do the show on birth order, so instead of warming up the audience with a comedian, they decided to have the audience seat themselves according to their birth orders.

When Leeza walked on stage, she introduced me and the subject and mentioned how they had divided the audience. She then said, "Where are you onlies?" There was polite applause.

"First borns?" Polite applause again.

"Middle borns?" A little quieter applause.

"Last borns?" You would have thought this group had just won the Super Bowl! They shouted, jumped up and down, and waved their hands like they were trying to flag down a plane on a deserted island.

Last borns frequently give away their birth order just by their names. If you meet a twenty-five-year-old "Robbie," you're probably meeting a last born. A first born would have insisted on being called "Robert" or "Rob" before he hit the job market after college. If you're introduced to an adult woman who goes by the name Krissy, Suzy, or Missy, you can bet you're talking to a baby.

A last born's favorite phrase might be, "I wonder what would happen if . . ." When you get the wedding photos back and see that one of the six-year-old crumb crunchers pulled his shirttail out of his fly, spoiling the portrait, two to one says he's a last born. When everybody else throws rice as the happy couple races down the sidewalk, the last born thinks, "What would happen if I throw gravel instead" (I actually pulled this stunt myself once—my dad showed me exactly what would happen, and it wasn't fun, though his discipline held me back the next time I asked myself, "What would happen if I threw rice pudding?")

As the performers, last borns tend to take far more risks than their conservative older siblings, but they are also less industrious, cherishing the idea of "play now, pay later." One exception: Some last borns can become very intense if it's a case of "I'll show them." Because they're often told that they're too young or too small or too dumb, last borns can become very ambitious to prove others wrong. But along the way, they still love being pampered and spoiled and rarely lose their affection for the spotlight.

This desire to be the center of everyone's attention can manifest itself in many ways. Maybe the child will become the class clown. Maybe she'll become the weak, slow one the family always has to wait for whenever they take family walks. Maybe he'll become the messie or the rebel—all these different behaviors have one end in mind: making adults notice the baby.

Vocationally, last borns are best suited for people-oriented jobs. Some babies could sell encyclopedias to illiterate families and make a pretty good living at it. I made a killing one summer selling magazine subscriptions, becoming the company's most successful salesman ever. That's because I learned to schmooze my way into the house where I could make my pitch. If I could make them laugh—and usually I could—more often than not they'd buy a magazine subscription.

Comfortable around people, last borns are frequently extroverts, energized by the presence of other people and good in relationships—affectionate, uncomplicated, and generally cheerful (as long as you give them their daily diet of attention). They make great friends and companions.

Their weaknesses include an attention span of about five seconds. Last borns hate to be bored almost as much as they hate to be rejected. If it's not fun, they want to do something else. They can be a bit self-centered and optimistic almost to a fault, which can get them into a lot of trouble. Babies have the troubling tendency to rationalize, as in, "I know I don't have the money to pay for this today, but if I put it on a credit card, I'm sure I'll have the money next week."

To first borns, last borns may seem undisciplined and gullible. In the wrong personality, the tendency toward attention seeking can become full-blown self-centeredness. Last borns sometimes play the role of the rebellious child; they can be temperamental and moody, spoiled and impatient. They frequently don't have time for unnecessary distractions like balancing a checkbook, putting their car keys someplace where they can find them, or picking up their room.

Though I've described last borns as the life of the party type of people, they also have a surprising ambivalence about them. That is, they can go from laughing and joking to crying and being moody in a matter of seconds. Researchers aren't sure why this is, but I have my own theory: The baby of the family can be coddled one minute, then berated the next. Though they are often treated as special by the parents, they are also frequently reminded by their older siblings that they are the runt, the weakling, or the stupid one. This can create an almost Jekyll and Hyde type of personality.

### The Middleman

I'm a proud supporter of the University of Arizona athletic program and have had the privilege of getting to know many of the coaches. Head basketball coach Lute Olson provided me with an interesting insight into his 1997 championship team: Two of the top eight kids were only children, five were first borns, and just one was a middle child—Mike Bibby, the star point guard who now plays in the NBA. Lute told me that Mike was one of the most coachable players he's ever had; as a middle born, Mike didn't have the ego that the other players had. The point guard's job is to be, quite literally, the middleman, the guy who keeps everything together, and Mike played that role perfectly.

Middles usually take on the temperament of a phlegmatic. They like peace at all costs. Middles are the negotiators, the mediators, and the compromisers. Looked at cynically, they might also be considered the brownnosers, because they don't like confrontation. They want everybody to get along, and they tend to have a strong fear of being the one who gets blamed.

Middle borns are the hardest to define because a middle can go in any number of directions. Most often that direction is directly opposite of the child just above them (the first born if the middle is a second born, the second born if the middle is a third born, and so on). If the first born is a star athlete, the middle might become a scholar. If the first born is a musician, the second born might drive motorcycles. In most instances, she is trying to carve out her own distinguishing personality, which means reacting away from the first born's path.

Occasionally, the second born may think he can outdo his older brother or sister—the way Donald Trump, Richard Nixon, and former President George Bush Sr. did—and more than one middle has been known to follow this path with gusto. But if the middle doesn't think he can surpass the first born's legacy, he'll usually react by trying to create his own.

Genders take on even more significance with middles. Middle-born boys who come from families in which all the children are boys tend to take on classic middle-born characteristics, but middle boys who have all female siblings may take on some first-born characteristics because they are the first-born male (the same is true for a middle female with all male siblings).

The classic middle born is usually a good team player and is reliable, steady, and loyal. There are exceptions, depending on age spacing. Sometimes a middle born will be a scrappy, ambitious climber just aching to pull down a first born, but that's not the norm.

Middles aren't as comfortable making decisions as are first borns. They have a higher degree of doubt than first borns and consequently tend to be less gifted at solving problems (though great as mediators or when solving disputes). They roll with the punches and are amiable, down-to-earth, and great at listening. They can be unselfish to a fault and very loyal. They're the nice, polite, laid-back, and usually nondescript type of people; they don't stand out in a crowd and don't make waves, but they are very pleasant to be around.

On the negative side, middle borns may have a difficult time setting boundaries. They may try to please everybody and, consequently, frustrate everyone in the process. When something goes wrong, they will sometimes take the blame, even when they are not at fault.

Here's the middle's dilemma: First-born Frank gets all the respect. He's the oldest, the smartest, and the biggest. Last-born Linda gets all the affection. She's the cutest, the smallest, and the one in need of most attention. Middle-born Mike gets squeezed out. He doesn't get the respect of the first born or the attention of the last born. In fact, what he most often gets is the blame. He can't out-argue Frank, and Linda gets excused because she's so little, so guess who has the finger pointing at him? And if Middle-born Mike ever gets so bold as to actually hit the little princess, he won't be able to sit down for a week.

While middles defy easy stereotyping, in general they tend to be more secretive than their other siblings. Their frequent history of getting blamed leads them to play their cards close to the vest, so to speak, and to think that others have it in for them. (Richard Nixon was a middle—enough said!)

Because they have had to forge their own way, middles are usually mentally tough and independent minded. They haven't been spoiled like the last born, and getting ignored means they learned early on that they have to make their own way. You won't see too many middles who hate the thought of moving out of their parents' house—they usually can't wait to get out on their own.

Middles make excellent marriage partners. In fact, they represent the most faithful of all birth orders. They may not be as fun as the last borns, or provide quite as well as the first borns, but they do tend to be very loyal, eager to please, and accommodating. They're sort of like a universal donor at the blood bank, because they fit in with everything.

Unfortunately, while one middle can be good, two middles married to each other can be disaster. In my counseling practice, I once talked to a couple of middle children who got married and who, in two years of marriage, had yet to consummate their vows. I sort of got a clue when the mother of the groom was the one who made the appointment. She knew somebody had to step in and do something. When I talked to this couple, I felt like I was talking to two kids on the playground—one was saying, "You start it," the other was saying, "No, you start it," and with both of them being middles, it just never got started!

As middles, both of them feared conflict even more than they wanted to enjoy sexual intimacy. If you're not a middle, you probably just can't understand that.

### The Prince in Waiting

You already know the first born. You probably voted for him to become president. Or maybe you work for her at a Fortune 500 company. Perhaps you watched him fly

48

into space as an astronaut, or you've read one of her best-selling books. All of these occupations are overwhelmingly populated with first-born adults.

First borns are pretty easy to spot: Every hair is in place, their clothes are immaculate, and their shoes are shined. Their cars are vacuumed, and they're the ones who buy the palm pilots and the day-timers (and who actually use them). You can count on them to be prompt, and their easygoing confidence is obvious by the way they shake your hand and look directly into your eyes.

I call first-born children adults in kids' bodies. They are known for being capable, hard driving, perfectionistic, exacting, exhaustingly logical (just get into an argument with one), scholarly, and organized. I know of one first-born pro golfer who is known for hanging his shirts in his closet according to the order in which he'll wear them. I'm not joking. Monday comes first, followed by Tuesday, then Wednesday, and so on. When a reporter asked him if this was really true, the golfer seemed surprised. "How else would I organize them?" he asked. It didn't even occur to him that a vast number of people never even think to organize their closets!

Though first borns like to be in charge, this desire for control can produce different results. Some first borns will be the Type A bosses who rule through power. Others will be the compliant nurturers who take care of the world as nurses or teachers. If the first born is raised by a critical parent, the child may learn that the way to get along is to be cooperative and easy to work with. Rather than taking charge, these first borns are best suited for middle management roles—they will get a task done, and they'll do it correctly, but they don't want to take the lead, and they won't rock the boat.

My wife is a compliant first born. She was once served a piece of salmon that was so raw it could have started swimming upstream if you put it in a river, but she refused to send it back—until her last-born husband, who doesn't have a compliant bone in his body, did the job for her.

First borns rarely fall far from the tree. If the parents are bleeding heart liberals, the first born would rather vote for Mickey Mouse than a Republican. If the parents are card-carrying conservatives, the first born is likely to be a member of the Ronald Reagan fan club.

Many first borns are very meticulous. Any profession that requires exactitude sounds good to them: airline pilots, accountants, astronauts, and the like all tend to be oldest children. If you need to get something done, if you want to start a business, if you're looking for someone to bring organization to chaos—in all these instances, you'll be best served by a first born.

### The One and Only

I call only children superfirsts. Take the best and worst qualities of a first born, magnify them two or three times, and you've just created the recipe for an only child. Not only are only children leaders, but they tend to be super-perfectionists. Everything is black and white, meaning, "Do it my way or the wrong way." Because of this, they tend to be critical and not a little selfish. They can some-times run over people and may have little regard for oth-ers' emotions.

More than likely, your typical only child is a list maker and scholar and thrives on logic. Only children tend to be very neat, but even the few messies know where to find something amid their piles. They are the megamovers of the world: task oriented, extremely well organized, very conscientious, and ultimately dependable. They love facts, ideas, and details and feel very comfortable with responsibility.

Only borns may be introverted. Though they enjoy one-on-one interactions, they have little patience for group small talk at social events. They are often unforgiving and very demanding. They hate to admit they're wrong and usually don't accept criticism well.

The special situation of only borns can create two different kinds of people. The first is the child who is seething underneath the surface. Always raised on a tightly structured, highly disciplined plan—expected to be and to act grown up from the time he is five years old, living around adults and often socializing primarily with adults—this child can be very cool and calm on the surface, but underneath he is very resentful of having to be a little adult who is cheated out of his childhood.

The other situation is the "crown jewel of the universe" syndrome. Both parents pour their love, energy, adulation, and financial resources into this child. She is the center of her parents' universe, is always made to feel superspecial, and never has to share her parents' affection with other siblings. The irony here is that some of these only borns may take on last-born traits.

Whatever the case, only borns are well represented among those who have accomplished much: T. Boone Pickens, Ted Koppel, Dr. James Dobson, Brooke Shields, Roger Staubach, Lena Horne, Joe Montana, Robin Williams, the late Steve Allen, and Lauren Bacall are just a few only borns who have made their mark on the world.

This is the one birth order that occasionally fools me during my seminars. I might peg someone as a baby of the family, but they'll proudly correct me: "No, I'm an only child!" When they say that, I can tell them a lot about their childhood and how they were probably quite spoiled growing up. In virtually all cases, they'll sheepishly admit that, yes, the house was sort of centered around them.

## When You're the Exception

Our daughter Lauren, who is nine as I write this, was born to us when Sande and I were forty-seven and forty-nine. We should have known something was up the first time we laid eyes on her. Sande and I have brown eyes; late-in-life Lauren popped out with green eyes and a CEO personality: "All right, world, I've arrived. Time to get everything in order."

Now you would think that this youngest of five children would end up being the family mascot, the cutesy little flopsy mopsy who is spoiled rotten and great at putting people in her service.

Nothing could be further from the truth.

You see, there's a large gap between Lauren and her next oldest sister, Hannah—over five years—making Lauren very much like an only child (albeit with at least six parents of whom we're aware). She is noted for saying things such as, "Well, I'll take that as a no," with her legs crossed demurely like a refined young socialite. I see her doing this sometimes and think, *Where did she come from?*

Lauren has a pet hamster named Sugar Foot, and pity the poor fool who visits our house and mentions Lauren's "gerbil."

"It's not a *gerbil!*" she'll tell you forcefully. "It's a *hamster.*"

We typically flee the hot oven known as Tucson near the beginning of June, finding refuge at a lake house near Jamestown, New York. Recently, as we prepared to make our annual pilgrimage, Lauren found a neighbor boy in Tucson who was willing to watch little Sugar Foot.

Like a typical only child would do, Lauren got out a big piece of construction paper and wrote out "Instructions for Sugar Foot." The colored paper contained no fewer than twelve very specific rules, covering Sugar Foot's physical as well as emotional well-being—"Stroke Sugar Foot's back softly, but be careful that you never spook him."

Reading over this very exhaustive list, I was struck by how thoroughly Lauren had done her job. Having read the twelve rules, I knew exactly how Sugar Foot should be cared for. Had I known nothing about this little girl, I would have assumed I was reading the work of an only born—and that's a point I want to make early on. Birth order can produce any number of exceptions, Lauren being a prime example.

Lauren's only-born tendencies were seen further over a topic that raised its head too many times to count. For a long time, Lauren loved her beyond-shoulder-length hair. Though I have said in many books and countless seminars, "Don't major in the minors," there was a time when it would have pleased my soul greatly if Lauren had consented to having her hair cut short. Lauren has nice thick hair, but it was getting way too long, well past her shoulders. (Keep in mind, we live in a hot area where coyotes start searching for lemonade in April.) Since summer was coming up, I thought it would be a good time for Lauren to think about getting a shorter style.

I offered up a steady barrage of innuendos and even straight-out suggestions: "Lauren, your hair is getting *so* long, sweetie." In a teasing way, I sometimes told her, "You know, when you're sleeping tonight, I could get some scissors and save you some money by cutting off your hair. You wouldn't feel a thing."

Lauren immediately grabbed her hair, as if I had the scissors in my hand that very moment, and said, "Oh, no, no, no, no, no, no."

Though I'm ashamed to admit this, I even bribed Lauren one day, promising to take her to that cheese-breath rodent place if she'd just consent to getting a more manageable hairstyle. No such luck.

So you can imagine my surprise when I recently walked into my house and discovered that Lauren had gotten her hair cut. It was wonderful, cut just below her ears and turned up on the ends.

I immediately said, "Lauren, I love your hair. It is absolutely adorable."

Lauren nodded but made sure I didn't make too much of it. "Dad," she said, "I only let the lady cut my hair because she agreed that she would do it exactly as I wanted it done. I told her it could be short as long as we flipped it up like one of the Dixie Chicks."

Think about it: A nine-year-old kid went out of her way to tell Sande and me that the only reason her hair was cut short was because it was done exactly the way she wanted it to be done. Only child, thy name is Lauren!

Except that Lauren is a last born. What's going on here?

A number of variables can readjust birth order. The order of your birth is significant and long lasting, but other factors contribute to who you are as well. In Lauren's case, spacing has made a big difference. Any gap of five years or more between siblings is significant. I know a young man whose two older siblings—both males—are eight and ten years older than him, and he has developed classic first-born tendencies as a result. For many years, he has met with an accountability group made up largely of middle-born guys, and they are practically ready to throw him out. His constant harping about doing it the right way and keeping everything on schedule and arguing over the most minor details has become very grating to the laid-back middles.

Lauren can't really remember living with her three older siblings—they were all out of the house before she turned five, and there are almost six years between her and Hannah—so in many ways she has adopted some only-child tendencies.

Another factor that bears mentioning is sibling gender. I referred to this briefly when talking about middle children. A quiet, reserved first-born female may have a very ambitious, first-born-oriented little brother, particularly if there are other siblings who follow. I know a family in which the first-born daughter is a compliant nurturer. She lives a very quiet, unambitious life and is happy at home. Her brother is a hard-charging, ambitious little boy, driven to excel in everything he does—and he wants to do a lot: scouts, sports, you name it. Being a first-born male or first-born female is significant, even if you are actually the third or fourth child.

Another factor includes physical, mental, or emotional differences. If an older sibling becomes ill or disabled (as was the case in Richard Nixon's family), the younger child can pass the older and take on first-born characteristics. Or the case may simply be that the second child is more naturally gifted and thus ends up overshadowing the older sibling, reversing the roles—and reversing the stereotypical effect of birth order.

Yet another factor to consider is the blender effect caused by sibling deaths, adoptions, or divorce and remarriage, all of which can shuffle traditional birth-order characteristics. That's just one of many reasons I urge single parents not to get remarried until their children are grown. Most young parents have no idea how earth-shattering it can be for a ten-year-old first born to lose a parent, then get a "replacement" along with a twelve-year-old sibling who unseats him as the first born.

There's one more factor that affects how you respond to birth order, and that's the order into which your parents were born. A first-born mom will run her home much differently, on average, than a last-born mom. The last-born mom will tend to be less strict about her children's eating and sleeping schedules (lunch may well be served at 2:00 P.M.), while the first-born mom will usually have a more orderly approach to child rearing. A middle-born dad will often value peace above all else, while a first-born dad may push all his children to achieve. Each one of these parenting styles will affect you to a different degree.

Perhaps the most devastating diverter of birth order is to have a critical parent. An unceasing barrage of antagonism will eventually wear down even the hardiest child, eroding the confidence of a first born or the "be happy" attitude of a last born. Criticism is like a personality virus; it can take the strongest personality and wipe it out.

For example, if you're a first born reading these pages, seeing yourself described as a leader, a scholar, a mover and shaker, and you see yourself as anything but; if you feel defeated, great at starting things but lousy at finishing them; if your expectations have sunk lower as the years have rolled by, you could well be what I call a "defeated perfectionist."

Although we don't have time to devote a whole section to this phenomenon, I comprehensively address the effect of critical parents in my book *When Your Best Isn't Good Enough*. I encourage you to pick up this book and read it, because you'll see how many people there are like you—so full of potential and so talented, but who have been decimated by the flaw-picking parent who *still* seemingly sabotages their every move. My hope is that when you read accounts of people who have overcome such a difficult start, you'll develop the skills necessary to achieve your full potential.

Now that you understand a bit more about the home environment that has shaped you so profoundly, we're going to spend some time in the next chapter examining a representative or two from each birth order, looking at how each person capitalized on their strengths, overcame their weaknesses, and reached their full potential.

# 4

## Making the Most
## of Who You Are

Without apology, I'm a huge basketball fan. I enjoy watching college games much more than I do the NBA, however, so I keep a close eye on the up-and-comers, particularly as they might relate to the University of Arizona.

In the mid-nineties, a very promising high school player named Taj McDavid looked like he had the world waiting at his feet. McDavid was the 1995–1996 South Carolina class AA player of the year, averaging twenty-six points and thirteen rebounds for Palmetto High School. At six feet six, McDavid had "college and pro prospect" written all over him. It looked like he could have a promising college career and a very real shot at turning pro.

Lawton Williams, McDavid's high school coach, had his doubts, however. According to *Sports Illustrated*, he said McDavid was certainly a gifted athlete, but that he had a "dubious work ethic."[1] Not helping his star player any, Williams added that McDavid had thrived against "mediocre competition."

College recruiters loved McDavid's stats, but they were wary of his poor grades. McDavid saw his college stock going down and ultimately decided to do what several high school seniors have done: He declared himself eligible for the NBA draft.

When a high school player signs on with an agent—as most do to declare for the draft—they make themselves ineligible to play college ball. The gamble has worked for some—Kobe Bryant, Kevin Garnett, and Tracy McGrady, to name just three—but in McDavid's case, it was a serious error. Not a single NBA team was interested. McDavid wasn't drafted, and because he had declared for the draft, he wasn't eligible to play college ball. His grades were too poor to get into most good colleges, and suddenly the man with a bright future was facing some very dark days.

What do you do when you bet your future on a dream, and the dream collapses? Without an opportunity to play college ball, McDavid has little chance of ever attracting NBA attention.

Can I be honest with you? I *hate* reading stories like this. It makes me sadder than you could know to see a young man with potential make a few bad decisions and end up running that potential into the gutter. Maybe I'm extra sensitive to this because I was so close to doing the same thing to myself.

That's why I really hope this book can help you make the most of who you are. I don't want you to show promise but then fizzle out. I want you to really think about what makes you the unique person you are, and then I want you to give some time and thought to how you can improve on that.

To do this, let's look at classic representatives of each birth order, exploring how birth order played a role in who they are and what they've done. I want you to see that it's possible to succeed no matter what your start in life.

## Will Rogers: The Legendary Last Born

Will Rogers, famous humorist, columnist, and actor, was born the last of seven children. When you've got six people ahead of you, you have to go *way* out of your way to get noticed. Will found a method that has worked for last borns for centuries: He became the life of the party. Explaining why he was last, Will writes, "I was the youngest and last of 7 children. My folks looked me over and instead of the usual drowning procedure, they said, 'This thing has gone far enough, if they are going to look like this, we will stop.'"[2]

Will's humor (natural for most last borns) is legendary. One of his most famous remarks took place at a fancy New York dinner. Each speaker was told to keep his words to eight minutes or less, but one speaker tortured the audience by droning on for forty-five minutes, finally concluding with, "Mr. Toastmaster, I'm sorry if I overstayed my time, but I left my watch at home."

Will leaned forward and said, "There was a calendar right behind you." The crowd erupted into delighted laughter and enthusiastic applause.

One time Will's sense of humor got him into trouble. No surprise there; most last borns are bound to create a few problems for themselves eventually. During a radio broadcast, Will announced a surprise guest, "The president of the United States, Calvin Coolidge." Will was a great impressionist, and he fooled a lot of people when he spoke in Coolidge's voice: "It gives me great pleasure to report on the state of the nation. The nation is prosperous on the whole, but how much prosperity is there in a hole?"

Some listeners who had been fooled were furious when they learned the truth, and some (no doubt, first-born) managers were apprehensive about how Coolidge would respond, but the president could take a joke and responded by inviting Will to dinner at the White House.

Just before Will was to meet the chief executive, a friend bet Will that he couldn't make the famously somber president laugh inside of two minutes. Will scoffed, replying, "I'll bet he laughs in twenty seconds." His friend eagerly took that bet.

Let me pause here to point out that only a last born would do this. Will was just about to meet the president of the United States for the first time, and what was he thinking about? How he could win a bet by making the president laugh in twenty seconds!

An official led the president in and said, "Mr. Coolidge, I want to introduce Mr. Will Rogers." Will offered his hand but looked confused. He finally broke the awkward silence by saying, "Excuse me, I didn't quite get the name."

Needless to say, Will won his bet.

The part I really like comes next: During the dinner, conversation soon turned toward Will's impersonation of the president. Mrs. Coolidge said that she thought there was only one person who did a better impersonation of Mr. Coolidge, and that was herself. After a short demonstration, Will applauded, then said, "Yes, that's mighty fine, Mrs. Coolidge. But think what you had to go through to learn it."

Will made a good living as a columnist, an actor, and a speaker. He's a classic last born, best known for his phrase "I never met a man I didn't like." Comedy is what made him famous, got him into trouble, and then got him out of trouble. He used his best qualities to create a name for himself and to go far.

His journey to success wasn't easy or automatic. In fact, like me, Will almost got himself kicked out of school—something about a runaway colt that Will skipped school to rope. The president of the school saw the runaway colt with Will's rope around its neck and thought he'd help. Unfortunately, the incident ended with the president flat on his back, threatening to expel Will.

When Will's parents heard the news, they were more than a little frustrated. Homer Croy, one of Will's biographers, writes, "[Will's] father was disturbed; in fact he was always disturbed about Will. The boy wouldn't study, he wouldn't work; all he wanted to do was to swing a rope, ride horses, or go visiting. Anything to have a good time. So his father thought it over . . . what could he do with the boy? His solution floored poor Will."

Military school!

Will got desperate to change his father's mind, but an incident soon after that sealed his fate. Keep in mind, Will was supposed to be on his best behavior to convince his dad that he didn't need military school. So what did he do? He started showing off to his friends by smoking a couple of cigars and throwing the match over his shoulder, as he saw older men do. Unfortunately, Will was a bit too young to realize that those men weren't throwing lit matches onto dry prairie grass. Almost instantly the field was on fire.

Neighbors pitched in to help put out the ensuing blaze, but they were as angry as Will knew his dad would be. Yet even in the midst of a crisis, Will didn't lose his sense of humor.

"What if we hadn't licked the fire, Willie?" one neighbor asked him. "What would you be doing?"

"I'd be ridin'," Will responded.

Will didn't last long at the military school. He quit, finally giving up school for good. No fewer than six schools had tried to tame him, and all of them had failed. Will knew he couldn't return home, so he went out on his own, getting odd jobs and doing the best he could. But he never lost his sense of humor. He owned two dogs and decided to name one "You Know" and the other "Did He Bite You?" That way, when a visitor asked the name of the dog, Will could say, "Did He Bite You?"

The visitor would say, "No, I just wanted to know his name."

Will would look sober and say, "You Know."

This could get people quite irritated, but Will didn't care. He thought it was very funny.

Will eventually got a part in the traveling "Texas Jack's Wild West Show" and continued to live a pretty wild existence through most of his twenties.

What helped turn Will around? The same thing that turned me around—a wonderful, refined young woman. In Will's case, her name was Betty Blake, described in her hometown newspaper as having taken a prominent part in the social life of the city. The notice goes on to call Betty one of the best known young ladies of Northwest Arkansas. Her attractive personal qualities made her a general favorite. Though quite shy (the first time Will saw Betty, he was so impressed he turned and ran), Will eventually got up the nerve to go courting.

Betty's family wasn't thrilled with Will. In their minds he was just a vaudeville player who roped a running horse on the stage. No future to that.

But they were shortsighted. With the stability of Betty in his life, Will put his theatrics to newer and better uses. He started acting in the new picture shows, kept doing his own shows, and before long his fame spread far and wide. During his day he was one of the most famous men in

America, known as a performer, writer, and much sought-after speaker.

Even as he became a celebrity, Will held on to those traits that helped him succeed. Croy states, "Will the great celebrity had exactly the same traits and characteristics he had had when he was a child. But now they were more marked. One was his ceaseless physical energy. Another was his friendliness. Another his interest in political affairs. Another was his honesty and integrity. And now, to these, was added his love of his family."

Most of these, you know by now, are classic last-born traits. Will put them to good use, allowed himself to be somewhat tamed by family life, and thus succeeded beyond his parents' wildest dreams. Will's father had wondered whether anything could ever come of such a troublemaker, but Will grew into a very influential, wealthy, and famous man. Even more important, he matured into a person of integrity and strong family.

Will died tragically in a 1935 plane crash. It was one of those deaths where everyone in his day could remember where they were when they heard the news. Dignitaries from around the world came to honor the last-born man who never met a man he didn't like.

And boy, they sure did like him back!

I want all you last borns to realize your dilemma: You have the power to make people laugh, to be the life of the party, and to be very persuasive. You can use it to show off by smoking cigars, getting kicked out of school, and making a general nuisance of yourself, or you can turn it around and use it to carve out a successful career in show business, sales, or something similar. I recommend you get a stabilizing influence in your life. It's probably best for you *not* to marry another last born. You need a Betty Blake or a Sande Leman—a down-to-earth person who can rein in your worst tendencies yet help you fan your best characteristics into flame. If you're a female last born, find a responsible, first-born husband. You may find him boring at times, but if you marry someone just like yourself, you're liable to get buried under chaos, unpaid bills, and a big mess. (I wrote about birth order and favorable marriage matches in *The Birth Order Connection,* also published by Revell.)

## Charlton Heston and Oprah Winfrey: First Borns Doing It Right

### Charlton Heston

Charlton Heston is the first of three children. As many first borns do, Heston spent a lot of time alone as a youngster. "I spent most of my time by myself in the woods, running a trapline with no success, and fishing and hunting. . . . All kids play pretend games, but I did it more than most. Even when we moved to Chicago, I was more or less a loner."[3]

Though he went into a profession largely populated by babies, Heston has maintained his first-born qualities. He's been on the forefront of social activism for decades, marching with Martin Luther King Jr. and being in the gallery when the Senate passed the Civil Rights Act. He traveled on behalf of the State Department on cultural missions to Nigeria and Egypt, was chairman of the American Film Institute, and joined four unions and helped found a fifth. He has been president of the Screen Actors Guild longer than anyone else ever has, and he continues to make headlines as the president of the National Rifle Association (NRA).

I've had the pleasure of meeting Charlton Heston, and his presence was regal. His voice is captivating; every word comes from a depth resembling a canyon, and his statements seem taken from granite. You don't dare question anything he says. The first question I asked him was,

"Are you a first born?" Heston responded, "Oh yes, very much so."

But if you didn't know about his leadership, you'd still probably pick up on his birth order from his comments. On one occasion, Heston saw fellow actor Robert De Niro in a restaurant. Although both are famous Hollywood actors, the two had never met before, and in their very first conversation, Heston said, "Mr. De Niro, we've not met, but I can't miss the opportunity to tell you that I think you're the best American film actor of your generation."

De Niro thanked him, then Heston continued, "But you have to do Shakespeare. Those are the best parts."

"People tell me that all the time," De Niro replied.

"They're right," Heston continued. "Those are the parts. If you don't do those parts, you're not in the game."

Heston saw from De Niro's face that he had irritated the younger actor, so he said, "I'm disturbing you. I apologize for that. But I'm right."

Did you catch that? Even in complimenting another actor with astonishing praise ("the best actor of his generation!"), first-born Heston had to tell De Niro how to do it just a little bit better. Though he knew he had irritated De Niro, he still insisted, "But I'm right."

Heston believes his experience as an actor has given him a disdain for people who lead undisciplined, sloppy lives. I think it's his birth order, but I'll let him have his say: "I have become closer to these dead guys who I've played than—I'm a different man than I would have been had I not played them. I think . . . there's also a possibility that my affinity with these guys has—dare I use the word *disdain?*—made me a little disdainful of people who don't do that. You're supposed to be on time. You're supposed to know your words. You're not supposed to [mess up]. Now, people [mess up] in this business all the time. We all do. But it distresses me when I do it. If I miss a line, which I don't very often, it irritates me terribly."

This perfectionism and lack of empathy for others who mess up is classic first-born behavior.

What's interesting is that as a young man Heston felt somewhat insecure. His family moved from his small town to the suburbs, where Heston was, by his own description, "a skinny hick from the woods, and all the other kids seemed to be rich and know about girls. . . . Discontented with who I was, I spent a lot of time pretending to be other people. In Chicago, there were movies to go to, so I could be Gary Cooper and Errol Flynn, which was fine with me."

Out of this insecurity Heston forged a spectacularly successful career in show business, acting in more than eighty movies and performing in Shakespeare's plays on screen more often than any other actor ever has.

Heston's fame had a very different hue than Will Rogers's. People loved to be around Will Rogers because Will made them laugh. They fell in love with the comedian. He was the world's cute little brother, so to speak.

Heston is on the opposite end of the spectrum. He doesn't make people laugh (he was in just one successful comedy); he wants to motivate them—thus his leadership in the NRA, his work with unions, and his marching on behalf of civil rights. His best-known movies are the serious dramas: *Ben Hur, The Ten Commandments, The Agony and the Ecstasy,* and *El Cid.* Because of his outspoken and somewhat conservative positions, Heston is adored by many and reviled by others.

Are you getting it? Both a last born and a first born went into show business, but they were respected and revered for very different things; their careers took very different tracks, and even their movies had a very different flavor. One became the man who made us laugh and like him; the other became a man who inspired us, occasionally angered us, and always moved us.

## Oprah Winfrey

Another classic first born is Oprah Winfrey. Get this: Oprah was nominated for an academy award for her work in *The Color Purple*. What a lot of people don't realize is that *The Color Purple* was Oprah's first movie. Isn't that just like a first born? You take up acting, get nominated for an academy award, and then go find something else to do—like become the wealthiest black female entertainer of all time.

Oprah knows success: Her daytime show has been number one for years, and when she launched her own magazine, it went right to the top—the most successful magazine debut ever. More recently, Oprah has launched a series of all-day seminars entitled "Live Your Best Life." The sixteen hundred seats in Baltimore—at $185 a pop, mind you—sold out in forty-seven minutes.[4] Not everything she touches turns to gold (the movie *Beloved* didn't fare so well), but if you could buy stock in a person, you couldn't do much better than placing a large percentage of your IRA in Oprah, Inc.

I've also met Oprah. In fact, I thoroughly embarrassed myself on her program. This was in the days before Oprah was OPRAH. She was generally well known but not a household name like she is today. During the first segment of the show, I kept referring to Oprah by her name, as I do with all hosts. I like to be friendly.

Well, imagine my chagrin when the producer walked up to me during the first break and said, "You're doing a really great job, Dr. Leman, but her name is 'Oprah,' not 'Ofrah.'"

Despite my mistake, Oprah must not have been too upset with me; she invited me back four times.

True to first-born form, Oprah doesn't just want to entertain—she wants to make a difference. "I don't have any particular hopes or dreams for the future," she told *Good*

*Housekeeping.* "I'm just a voice trying to help people redis-cover their best selves." In an article she wrote herself, Oprah states, "I want my work, all my work—movies, books, television—to be a light in people's lives." To that end, in 1998 Oprah took her audience of over twenty mil-lion on a self-improvement exercise, calling her program "Change Your Life TV."

This theme pervades Oprah's work. In a 2000 com-mencement address at Roosevelt University in Chicago, Oprah told the graduates, "There is a sacred calling on each of our lives that goes beyond this degree you're about to receive. There is a sacred contract that you made, that I made with the Creator when we came into being. Not just the sperm and the egg meeting when we came into the essence of who we were created to be. You made a con-tract, you had a calling. And whether you know it or not, it is your job to find out what that calling is and get about the business of doing it."

Oprah's horrific childhood is well known: Though a first born, she had little privilege. She was born into a very poor family, was sexually abused and raped, and gave birth to a child at fourteen (the child died). Her longtime friend Gayle King marvels at what Oprah has become, given her poor start: "It's a wonder she's not off in a cor-ner drooling."

First borns are often scholarly; at the very least, they usually have a few books on their bedside table, and Oprah is a well-known friend of books. She describes her ideal weekend as gobbling up three books and staying in her pajamas. Oprah's Book Club has almost single-handedly revitalized the publishing industry, particularly for nov-els, practically guaranteeing the chosen books a place on the national best-seller list.

In fact, books had a big role in helping Oprah overcome her difficult start. She said, "For me, getting my library card was like getting American citizenship." Just as Will

Rogers rode his humor and Charlton Heston rode classic movies, Oprah rode her books, as Ron Stodghill wrote in *Time*, "using the iron-willed protagonists she found in black literature to fire her dreams of rising beyond the back-breaking work that seemed the destiny of most of the black people she knew."

Like my first-born wife, Oprah is a pleaser. She once regaled a Baltimore audience with stories about her "disease to please." Not all first borns are pleasers but a number of them are. Oprah has talked about how this need to please used to hold her back until she reined it in. "Years ago, when I was running myself crazy trying to please everybody, I told Sidney Poitier it didn't matter how hard I worked, I couldn't seem to do enough to live up to other people's expectations, and he said, 'That's because you're carrying their dreams. What you have to do is find out what you expect of yourself and learn to live with that.' That really helped me a lot. I had to let go of other people's expectations and learn to live from the purest part of myself."

Though a pleaser, Oprah still likes to be in control—another typical first-born trait. She still signs all checks over $1,000 for her business, Harpo Entertainment Group, and meticulously scrutinizes the smaller ones that others sign for her. She binds employees at all levels to strict, life-long confidentiality agreements. And she guards her off-air ventures as fiercely. When Hearst (the publisher of *O* magazine) planned to coposition Oprah's first magazine issue with *Cosmopolitan* magazine by putting the two publications together in one special display, Oprah got on the phone and made them stop: "I am not going to be used to sell one of your other magazines," she said. "*Cosmo* is not who I am."

Though somewhat controlling, Oprah is extremely good to her staff. She likes to take them shopping, and from having been on her show I know that her assistants would do just about anything for her. Oprah is very loyal and expects 100 percent loyalty in return. If you want to get on her bad side, just violate her confidence—you're gone. The only gig you'll get after that is to appear on the *Jerry Springer* show.

In the book *Legends,* Maya Angelou wrote a moving tribute to Oprah: "She was born poor and powerless in a land where power is money and money is adored. Born black in a land where might is white and white is adored. Born female in a land where decisions are masculine and masculinity controls. This burdensome luggage would seem to indicate that travel was unlikely, if not downright impossible. Yet among the hills of Mississippi, the small, plain black girl with the funny name decided that she would travel and that she would do so carrying her own baggage."

Perhaps without realizing it, Angelou goes on to mention that behind Oprah's startling success is her role as America's big sister: "She is everyone's largehearted would-be sister, who goes where the fearful will not tread."

This is a great label. Everything Oprah does, millions want to copy. We read the books she recommends. We listen to the guests she invites into her studio. And even when she does something crazy, like run a marathon, we follow. Maybe it's a coincidence that the year after Oprah ran her marathon in Washington, D.C., marathon attendance increased 15 to 20 percent, but Oprah's trainer, Bob Greene, doesn't believe that: "[Oprah] has a tremendous effect on people. . . . Over the years she's been willing to go public with her life and her struggles, and people identify with her." I think we're just eager to follow our big sister.

Many women's respect for Oprah is so great that once when Oprah went into a public bathroom, people began lining up outside her stall, waiting for her to get out. When she finally reappeared, they applauded. A successful flush!

Oprah found her strength in reaching out to help others. She has gladly accepted the role of America's big sister.

Instead of letting herself be buried by bitterness, she put her traits to use to help others—and it's come back to bless her. Oprah told a *Newsweek* reporter of one incident in which a man stopped her just to thank her for her impact: "I think it really is an amazing accomplishment that I, who grew up a little Negro child who felt so unloved and so isolated—the emotion I felt most as a child was loneliness—and now the exact opposite has occurred for me in adulthood. Usually people just move through the future carrying the weight of their past. But for me, things have come absolutely full circle. I feel embraced by people's love. I think that is a tremendous gift."

Notice how both first borns, Charlton and Oprah, felt a great deal of loneliness growing up, but they used that stinging sense of alienation to push them into changing the world. Most last borns don't feel lonely, so they often lack the drive experienced by first borns.

First borns could learn a lot from Charlton's and Oprah's example. You may never be the life of the party. You might rub some people the wrong way. But you can get a lot done, more than last borns could ever dream about. You will have your own struggles to overcome—loneliness, perhaps, or a tendency to please others if you're one of the compliant first borns—but if you'll face these obstacles head-on, there's little you can't do. You were born to succeed.

## Tiger Woods: The Only One

Remember when I called only borns "superfirsts"? Perhaps no one has showcased this as much as Tiger Woods. In all of sports, I don't think I've seen anyone inspire such awe from fellow competitors. NBC analyst Johnny Miller, himself one of the best golfers ever, said, "[Tiger] is human, just barely."[5] Tiger has achieved a level of excellence that is so far beyond anyone else that writers are running out of metaphors to describe him.

Although Tiger's father has three other children from a previous marriage, Tiger was raised as an only child, and it shows. He appeared on national television in 1977 when he was just two years old, performing a putting exhibition on the *Mike Douglas Show*. A few years later, as a five-year-old, he was featured on *That's Incredible*. Tiger's high school golf coach noticed an only born's drive in Tiger right away: "Inside of him, there is a work ethic that most don't have. . . . Tiger Woods was the hardest working 13- or 14-year-old kid I've ever seen, as far as hitting golf clubs."

Earl Woods, Tiger's father, insists that Tiger's drive doesn't come from him as a parent. "[Tiger] is totally self-motivated. He pushes me, not me push him." Though I don't know Earl, what he's suggesting would not be uncharacteristic for an only born like Tiger.

Jack Nicklaus has noticed this same drive: "Tiger seems to have the mentality that when he gets three shots ahead, he wants to get six shots ahead, he wants to get ten shots ahead, he wants to get twelve shots ahead. I never really did that." Of course not, Jack—you're not an only born!

Pete McDaniel, a senior writer at *Golf Digest*, mentions Tiger's fierceness on the golf course: "Tiger will cut your hand off to beat you. He is that intense. He lives to be number one. He lives to win."

That helps to explain why Tiger has done so many things that have never been done before. His fifteen-stroke victory in the 2000 U.S. Open is the largest margin of victory in any of golf's four majors—ever. He is just the fifth player to win all four major championships and the first to hold all of them at the same time, something that Jack Nicklaus calls "the greatest golfing feat in modern time."

It's fun reading the accounts of reporters trying to find new ways to write about this phenomenon called Tiger Woods. The week of the 2001 U.S. Open, as Tiger was competing for his fifth straight major, Christine Brennan, writing for *USA Today*, went so far as to suggest that Tiger and God have a unique partnership. You see, Tiger was uncharacteristically struggling through the first nine holes, and his play wasn't getting any better. If you've ever played golf, you can relate—sometimes you just have bad days. Your swing doesn't show up.

Brennan suggested that God himself came to the rescue: "But then the wind and the rain and the lightning and the thunder came, and we found out there is one more golf fan in this great big world of ours than we originally thought. You Know Who hated seeing Tiger in this state, so forlorn and playing so poorly, so He stopped the action and let Woods escape Southern Hills just before he ballooned to 4-over par."

Obviously, the writer is having fun, but it still makes my point: No other athlete would be given this treatment. It would seem bizarre if a writer were to suggest that God caused an earthquake so that Shaquille O'Neal wouldn't embarrass himself at the foul line; nobody would get it if a sportswriter suggested that a hurricane hit because Pedro Martinez was about to walk a batter in the major leagues. What's funny about this article is that Christine Brennan can write it, and we can all laugh, because it almost seems plausible!

In fact, to give you an idea of just how amazing Tiger's game has become, Brennan talked about the weather warning signs that began popping up as Tiger's game was underway. The rules insist that at the first sign of possible lightning, fans have to clear the grandstands. People die from lightning strikes on a golf course almost every year, so it's a warning that is not to be taken lightly. When the officials tried to clear the bleachers at hole number seven, the fans wouldn't budge!

The officials couldn't believe it. These fans understood the very real threat of a lightning strike, but they wouldn't move. Brennan writes, "Thus we found out something new about the American sports fan. He or she would rather get hit by lightning than miss a chance to see Tiger up close."

As an only born, Tiger has no fear of other competitors. He grew up with a strong sense of entitlement, and he doesn't see any reason anybody else could ever beat him. That gives him a tremendous psychological advantage—and it shows. During his 2001 win in the Master's tournament, Tiger took a tense situation and blew it open with a move that dripped self-confidence. Golf writer Dan Jenkins wrote about it this way: "Here's a guy with a slender one-stroke lead for the Masters, for the modern Slam. So what does he do? He takes out the old driver and flirts with severe tragedy—the trees on the right—but confidently busts it 327 yards, around the corner, uphill, leaving himself nothing more than a 78-yard pitch shot to the pin. Pure gravy that he holed the birdie putt to win by two. He clinched it back on the tee with his talent and nerve."

As an only born, Tiger isn't likely to slow down any time soon. Pete McDaniel laughs, "[Tiger] will never rest on his laurels. Right now as we're speaking, he's probably hitting golf balls, trying to improve, trying to learn another shot."

Earl Woods has talked about how Tiger will become the next "Gandhi," ultimately changing the world. I wouldn't put it past Tiger. He has the right birth order, and he certainly has the motivation. Because Tiger is multiracial—white, black, Chinese, American Indian, and Thai descent—he was once tied to a tree in kindergarten and taunted mercilessly. I don't think it's a coincidence that early commercials featuring Tiger played up how Tiger used to be ineligible to play certain golf courses because of his color. With the strong influences of this experience and his birth order, there's no telling what Tiger might accomplish.

What only borns often lack, however, is the ability to cut back and enjoy a family. Some of Tiger's friends have suggested that there's no way he'll get married before thirty. If Tiger does get married, however, I'd warn him that the very thing that has made him so successful on the golf course is the same thing that will destroy his family. His drive, his demand for control, and his perfectionism will all work against him relationally.

If you're an only born, it's okay to set out to change the world. Your drive to succeed and achieve a rare state of excellence will inspire all of us. But do yourself a favor— let your hair down a little. Learn to enjoy life in the process. Find a loving man or woman who can make you laugh now and then. We all know there are things in this world that need to be changed, but this world also needs people who enjoy it. We don't have to sacrifice one for the other.

### David Letterman and Anne Morrow Lindbergh: Middle Children Fighting for Respect

#### David Letterman

David Letterman, a middle child (second of three), is in the same profession as Oprah Winfrey, Charlton Heston, and Will Rogers. There are a few differences—talk show hosts as opposed to movie actors—but in general they're part of the entertainment industry.

While last borns like Will Rogers and Julia Roberts can become universally loved for their work and their likable nature, and first borns like Oprah Winfrey and Charlton Heston will seek to change the world, middle borns in Hollywood will, more often than not, be fighting for respect. That certainly has been the case with David Letterman.

The most vivid example of birth order taking center stage occurred in the early nineties, as Johnny Carson retired and Jay Leno was chosen to replace him as host of *The Tonight Show.* For years Letterman was seen as the prince in waiting, the comedian expected to get the biggest job in television on the longest-running show in history. He was clearly Johnny Carson's choice (Johnny is also a middle born, by the way).

Interestingly enough, Jay Leno is a last born with classic last-born tendencies. According to one journalist, "At one point in his life Jay thought he would be a funny insurance salesman."[6] Jay developed his humor early on. He was mildly dyslexic and compensated by providing his friends and teachers with laughs. His fifth-grade teacher wrote out a report card that is typical for a last born: "If [Jay] used the effort toward his studies that he uses to be humorous, he'd be an A student. I hope he never loses his talent to make people chuckle."

In order to get the *Tonight Show* job, Jay worked the system. He was a great last-born schmoozer, so he did special presentations for local NBC affiliates, gave lots of interviews to local papers, and did all the PR stuff to get his name out there. He also did crazy things like hiding in a closet to hear conversations about who was going to be chosen, and he admittedly went out of his way to politick and campaign for the coveted spot. Babies are born manipulators, and they love the thrill of the chase, so it's not a surprise to me that the last born won the game.

Middles tend not even to play, which Letterman himself admits. When told that Leno said, "I like the game," Letterman responded, "I didn't know there was a 'game' involved in this. Or I don't acknowledge it or I don't play it." One writer pointed out that Letterman was "too polite to grease his own ascension." Letterman explains, "I just like to think that if you work really hard and do a really nice show, people will like you. Ha. Ha. And then, 16 years later, you find out: not necessarily!"

Like most middles, Letterman tends to be pretty secretive, which doesn't match his profession all that well. When Bill Carter, who wrote a book on the Leno-Letterman battle to succeed Johnny Carson, appeared on Tom Snyder's talk show, Letterman called in, disguising his voice and taking on the persona of a trucker, rambling about any number of issues. He later told another reporter that his sole purpose for the call, which seemingly went on forever, was to keep the book writer from talking about him as long as possible. "I just didn't want to hear them talking about that [stuff]," he told writer and friend Bill Zehme.

Letterman might seem eccentric to others, but I see a middle born trying to make it in a last born's world. Letterman has hired a worker whose job is to clear the corridors as he passes so that no one can look at him or stop him to talk. And he still can't see himself as successful. He was on the deck of a spectacularly beautiful Malibu beach home once, looking off into the Pacific Ocean, when he said wistfully, "I wish I could have something like this."

His host looked at him with astonishment. "Dave," he replied, "you *can*." Zehme explains, "Luxury embarrasses him; he prefers to believe himself undeserving. That he reportedly earns . . . [millions of dollars] per year does not register at all. In his mind, he dwells but a heartbeat away from failure and ruin."

Though it might sound tough to say this, while Letterman has been very successful, I'm not surprised he has had a rough go of it. He's a middle born doing a job tailor-made for a last born. His former producer admitted as much: "[Dave is] basically the same guy up until show time," says Robert "Morty" Morton. "Then he assumes a different personality for that hour, but afterward he's right back again." While middles can rise above their birth order, they're still going to pay a price for stepping out onto unfamiliar, and certainly uncomfortable, ground.

James Wolcott, writing for *The New Yorker,* analyzes Leno and Letterman this way:

On any given night, the difference between Letterman and Leno isn't one of talent or material but one of temperament. Leno . . . is a Las Vegas vending machine of predictable jokes. Letterman is less containable. . . . Letterman has flared up over technical flubs and miscues that have dragged out the taping of his show, and has indulged in acts of self-loathing bordering on masochism, the most blatant example being the time he pummeled a life-size dummy of himself on the air, giving it repeated shots to the head. His neurosis has achieved classical dimensions. I happened to be reading Dr. Karen Horney's "The Neurotic Personality of Our Time" recently, and (except for the pages that reminded me of me) almost every chapter cried out, *Dave, Dave, Dave.*

Though Wolcott doesn't use this language, what he's essentially saying is that Leno is a typical last born, and Letterman is a fairly typical middle born. He remarks, "It's questionable whether [Dave] can ever be happy on the air, given his irreconcilable desires to be the magnetic center and to be left . . . alone"—classic middle-born behavior.

What's funny is how Letterman tries to remake his job in the mold of a middle. He told one journalist, "Every day is a compromise." Just about every middle child will take on that attitude; I've never heard a last born say that. Another writer described Letterman as "America's great leveler."

Also like many middles, Letterman seems to be pretty loyal. When the time came for him to shake things up and actually fire someone, he did it in classic middle-born style. "Because we'd never done it before, we took our time, and we ended up counseling these people, and it went on and on. And at the end of the day . . . we were just limp, we were exhausted, it was a horrifying situation."

It was also a situation you won't find many first borns or last borns getting into. In fact, Dave can take this almost to an extreme. When a woman was arrested and prosecuted

for stalking him in a rather scary fashion, the public pros-
ecutor insisted that Dave was never "vindictive. He wanted
her to get help." A last born like me would have wanted a
crazy person like that to be locked up (and have the key
thrown away!).

Even in their disloyalty, middles can be loyal. Merrill
Markoe, one of Letterman's former girlfriends, came out
with a self-help book and actually appeared on one of
Dave's shows to promote it. The two hadn't spoken in six
years. Letterman explains why he was willing to have her
appear on his show: "Looking back at the end of that relationship, it was so unpleasant and mostly my fault. You
know, I don't know how to do things with women. She
was so good and so smart and just so decent, so I feel like,
if there's anything I can ever do for her, I would do it nine
times. I just don't know how to behave, you know? I don't
know how you break up with people."

This loyalty inspires loyalty. In spite of the fact that Leno
took over Carson's old show, Johnny spent the next year
making three appearances on Letterman's show without
appearing on Leno's show once.

I want you to take note of Letterman's expectations of
failure, self-loathing, and discomfort with the spotlight,
and see if you can't see any similarities in the life of another
middle-born celebrity, Anne Morrow Lindbergh.

### Anne Morrow Lindbergh

In a day when seemingly everyone gets their fifteen minutes of fame, it's difficult to imagine just how famous
Charles Lindbergh was in the early part of the twentieth
century. Before television, celebrities were much rarer, and
Charles's solo transatlantic flight made him the most liked,
popular, and respected man on the face of the earth. There
was really no comparison. Those of you under forty-five

may never understand the celebrity worship Charles Lindbergh received.

Charles's future wife, Anne Morrow, was the second of four children. A childhood breakfast ritual reveals that Anne was a middle child through and through. Every morning, after kissing their father, the Morrow kids would sit down for breakfast, and each one would be asked the same question by their father: "Who do you like best, your mother or your father?"

Elisabeth, the oldest child, was confident and direct. Looking her father straight in the eye, she said, "I like Mother best—and *next* to Mother I like you."

This response always made Mr. Morrow laugh and Anne start to quake, for she knew the question would be asked of her next. Dorothy Herrmann, Anne's biographer, writes, "To Anne, tensely awaiting her turn, it was obvious that he admired her sister's blunt honesty and didn't seem hurt at all. Yet Anne was timid and retiring by nature, a person who liked to remain in the background, placate people, and keep the atmosphere pleasant, while Elisabeth was her opposite—practical, independent, and fearless."[7]

In other words, Elisabeth was a first born, and Anne was a middle.

The biographer continues with Anne's father speaking: "Now, Anne, it's your turn. Who do you like best, your mother or me?"

"I like you both the same," Anne said quickly.

"Now, Anne, tell me the truth. Who do you love best?" he persisted, smiling.

"But I like you . . . *differently!*"

A middle born all the way!

According to Herrmann, Anne remained acutely aware of the differences between her and her sister. I think you middle-born females will be able to relate to this:

As is often the case with sisters, there was a strong, unspoken sibling rivalry between the two oldest girls. Anne did not consider Constance, who was seven years younger than herself, much of a threat, but she was painfully aware of the differences between Elisabeth and herself. Not only was Elisabeth smart, sophisticated, and witty, but she was a strikingly attractive blonde with an appealing ethereal quality. . . . She was somewhat taller than Anne, who had inherited her mother's plain looks and her father's tiny stature. As they grew older and began to date, Anne felt sure that men would prefer Elisabeth.

Because Mr. Morrow was so well connected, it was only a matter of time before his family welcomed Charles Lindbergh as their guest. Lindbergh was larger than life at the time, and Anne found herself in personal agony as she watched her older sister effortlessly make a grand impression.

Although Anne longed to say something charming and brilliant that would attract the attention of this celebrated young man, she sat tongue-tied with embarrassment as she listened to her older sister converse easily with him. It didn't seem fair, she told herself, that handsome men always brought out the best in Elisabeth while they terrified her and made her feel more awkward and childish than ever.

Anne wrote in her diary that she was certain Lindbergh would turn all his attention to Elisabeth.

[Charles] will turn quite naturally to E., whom he likes and feels at ease with. I will back out more and more, feeling in the way, stupid, useless and (in the bottom of my vain heart) hoping that perhaps there is a mistake and that I will be missed. But I am not missed. They never notice and become more and more interested in each other and you must be more and more careless and happy, although *you notice* every little thing, and you have long sessions

with yourself stamping out the envy, persuading yourself
it is only fair and right.

Charles did notice Elisabeth, and the two began seeing
each other. Anne talked with her younger sister Constance
about how grand a wedding Charles and Elisabeth would
have, planning it to the last detail.

Much to Anne's surprise, however, Charles and Elisabeth broke up. Even more surprising, Charles turned his
attention toward her! Anne wasn't sure how to take this.
"The myth of Charles Lindbergh, the handsome, daring
young American who was the most admired man in the
world, still dazzled her, and she couldn't quite believe that
of all the women in the world, including her beautiful,
socially adept older sister, he had picked her as his date."

It's not that Anne didn't have any concerns about the
desirability of Charles. In fact, she had plenty. Charles was
about as unlike Anne as someone could be. Anne was book-
ish, with a poetic soul, from a well-to-do background.
Charles came from a more blue-collar experience; he had
little time for books, and he liked to play what to Anne
seemed like tasteless practical jokes. Anne confided to her
sister Constance, "He never opens a book, does he? How
that separates him from our world! It is hideous to think
about—a hideous chasm. Do you ever think we could
bridge it and get to know him well? Oh I'm afraid—terribly afraid. I do not want to see him again. It is terribly upsetting, liking someone so utterly opposed to you."

What Anne didn't realize then (but what she would find
out later) is that finding someone *unlike* you is the key to
a great marital match. She finally received Charles's attention and then agreed to become his wife. The agreement
came at a great cost: Charles brought his secretive and literary middle-born fiancée into a public spotlight so bright
that they had to go to ridiculous lengths to avoid reporters
and photographers. Anne was whisked out of her wedding

in a borrowed car, lying down in the back to avoid being followed by reporters and photographers. People rented rooms next to them to listen in on their private conversations, and maids were bribed to disclose the most personal of details. The public couldn't get enough of Lindbergh and his new wife.

Before getting married, Anne had started to publish some well-received articles, but now even this had to be revisited. Charles warned her to "never say anything you wouldn't want shouted from the housetops, and never write anything you would mind seeing on the front page of a newspaper."

Anne later reflected: "I was convinced I must protect him and myself from intrusion into our private life, but what a sacrifice to make never to speak or write deeply or honestly! I, to whom an experience was not finished until it was written or shared in conversation. I who had said in college that the most exciting thing in life was communication. . . . The result was dampening for my kind of inner life. I stopped writing in my diary completely for three years and since even letters were unsafe, I tried to write cautiously or in family language and jokes."

To make matters more difficult for our eager-to-please middle born, Charles was not an easy man to live with. His daughter once said that there were only two ways of doing things—Charles's way and the wrong way. Yet it was also a marriage that released Anne from the worst tendencies of middle borns. Anne recounted, "As a married woman, I had my husband at my side and developed a new confidence. I always feel like standing up straight when he is behind me."

Somehow Charles gave Anne the confidence she lacked naturally. Instead of feeling like a pale comparison of her older sister, Anne was able to step out and carve a life of accomplishment from the opportunities brought her way. Anne became the first U.S. woman to get a glider pilot's license, and in 1934 the National Geographic Society awarded her the Hubbard Gold Medal for distinction in exploration, research, and discovery—the first woman ever to receive this award. In the later period of her life, Anne returned to writing, and her life experiences provided a new depth that rocketed her onto the best-sellers list in the 1950s and 60s.

You don't see a lot of middle borns on best-sellers lists. You don't see a lot of middle borns becoming exploration pioneers either. But Anne used the best of her birth order to accomplish the most.

It began with her relationship to Charles, of course. Though no one knows why Charles and Elisabeth broke up, I suspect, from Charles's strong-willed nature, that another first born simply wasn't a suitable mate. Charles and Elisabeth likely fought over the smallest details. The more placating Anne was a much better match. Anne would be loyal, and her desire to please would lead her to do and try things that other frailer women might shrink from.

You may have noticed a pattern in these life stories. Tiger Woods, the only born, is single. The first borns— Oprah Winfrey and Charlton Heston—don't have spouses who figure prominently into their stories (Oprah isn't even married, though she has a longtime companion). But Will Rogers, the last born, and Anne Morrow Lindbergh, the middle born, both benefited greatly from making a wise marital choice. I think David Letterman also would have benefited from a more stable relationship.

The key is to take a survey of your strengths and weaknesses, find a field of endeavor that fits who you are and how you see the world, and then throw yourself into it with abandon. You can succeed by breaking a few rules— Letterman in show business, for instance—but you'll also likely pay a price for doing so.

Whether you're born first, second, third, fourth, or eleventh, you can succeed; you just need to know who you are, build on your strengths, be aware of your likely weaknesses, and learn to overcome them. I hope you've been motivated to look a little deeper into who you are, particularly as it relates to your family of origin.

In the next chapter, we'll talk more about how to make the most of your birth order.

# 5

# Making Sense of Birth Order

Recently I picked up Hannah and Lauren from helping out at a local vacation Bible school for three- and four-year-old tots. Both of my daughters were volunteering, and each day I was greeted with, "Dad, my legs are *so* sore from having those babies on my lap" (from Lauren), and "Dad, you wouldn't believe what little Chloe did today!" (from Hannah).

On the final day, several of the adult leaders came up to me and said, "Dr. Leman, I just want you to know what a joy it was to have Lauren and Hannah here to help out. They came in every day, knew exactly where to go, got their assignment, and then they did it! On top of all that, when you put them together, you'd never know they were sisters by the way they get along so well."

All right, I know what you're thinking: "Hey, Leman, what's up? I thought kids who are next to each other in birth order are supposed to be night and day different! How come your two kids get along so well?"

Hannah and Lauren are very different in some respects, but they also get along extremely well. The age gap between them removes a lot of the competition Sande and I witnessed among our three older children.

Having had what almost amounts to two separate families, I've softened some of my earlier words about birth order. It's easy to make blanket statements—all babies are the same, all first borns run over people—but experience has shown me that birth order is not always so clearly defined. Many people come up to me after a seminar, as one woman did, to say, "Dr. Leman, I see a couple different birth orders at work in my personality."

"If you see a couple different birth orders, you might be a blend," I responded.

"What's that?"

"Well, let's take a look at your family."

"I'm the youngest, with an older sister and three older brothers."

"You're from a large family—that's usually where you see the most blends. As the baby, by the time you came along you had veteran parents, which can also affect birth order tendencies, but I'm guessing that a number of traditional birth order elements are still part of your personality."

"Like what?"

"Well, since you're the youngest, and your older sister is so much older, I'm guessing that by the time you were a toddler, your older sister was sort of like a second mom."

"Yeah, she really was—I wanted to be just like her. She was a librarian, and I always wanted to be a librarian."

"I'm also willing to bet that you were treated differently than your brothers were."

"How so?"

"Did you ever hear your mom say, 'the girls'?"

"Not very often; because of the age gap we didn't do all that much together."

"That's what I thought; you were seen as individuals. Now how many times were your three brothers referred to as 'the boys'?"

"All the time."

"They were a unit, weren't they? You've got the oldest, the middle, and little schnooky. And I bet most of them follow traditional birth-order patterns."

"They really do. My oldest brother does kind of act like the first born, and I can see my next oldest brother being the family peacemaker."

"Now, tell me, what brother did you have the most difficulty getting along with?"

"That's easy—my youngest brother."

"I'm not surprised by that, but why do you think that is, now that you've heard me talk about birth order?"

"Well, he was treated like the youngest born in some ways, since he was the youngest boy, but . . ."

"But he didn't get the privileges of the last born once you came along?" I finished for her.

"That's right."

"Do you see how he might have resented that? You sort of usurped him as the baby. In a family of just three boys, he'd have your pride of place."

It was like a little light blinked on behind her eyes. "Now I see; yeah, he often told me that he resented me. Now I know why. I guess I still really am a product of my environment."

"The good news is, with three older brothers, you probably feel very comfortable around men."

"I do."

"Allow me to let you in on a little secret: Men love it when women understand them as males. You've got a perfect background to have a very enjoyable marriage."

"That's encouraging!"

The good news is that if you've learned to become the product of your environment, you can unlearn the negative aspects and build on the positive aspects. In the case of this woman, I wanted her to see why she and her youngest brother had so much conflict—but I also wanted her to begin thinking about how having brothers could prepare her for a happy and successful life.

Maybe part of your personality is really working—we want to build on that. But maybe there's one side of you that is starting to wear more than just a little thin, at least from the perspective of your friends and family members. We want to change that.

Now that I'm closer to sixty than to fifty, I've had enough time to see how some of these personalities work their way out. Many years ago, I remember talking to a mother who had an unusually compliant first born. This was the type of baby who slept through the night, who laid docile and calm on the changing table while her diapers were being changed, and who practically thanked her mother for putting her down for her nap times.

Seeing this woman hold her newborn second child, I couldn't resist telling her, "Do you realize what that little boy is going to be like?"

She looked at me like I was crazy. How could I know? This baby was less than six months old! "No, not really."

"He's going to be Attila the Hun. You've already raised one saint, and that little sucker's gonna find out soon enough just what he has to do to get the same attention."

She was skeptical, assuming that the compliance of her first child was due entirely to her and her husband's innate parenting skills. As it turned out, I was right. That boy grew up to be as different from his sister as rugby is from chess.

Fast-forward a number of years—the boy is now a teenager, in my counseling office after having gotten himself into one scrape after another. The parents think he must be demon possessed or something. After all, they had already proven that they could raise one angel, so where did this devil come from? He was solely responsible for his parents' decision to have just two children—they didn't want to risk having another child like him.

When I walked the young man through his family and the pressures he must have felt growing up with such a perfect, compliant sister, he was finally able to see, for the very first time, the force to which he had been reacting all his life.

"You wanted to be noticed," I explained. "That's natural. But you couldn't be noticed by doing what your sister had already done—being inordinately cooperative and good. All that was old hat. If you were going to get your parents' attention, you'd have to find an entirely different route—you'd have to cause trouble."

I could see him nodding. Knowing he was ready for the next question, I slipped in, "So tell me, is it working for you?"

"Is what working for me?"

"Is the rebel role giving you what you want? Do you like getting suspended from school, having lowlifes for friends, being on a first-name basis with the local cops, and having a future that, at best, puts you working the pumps at the local Texaco for the rest of your life?"

"That's not what I want," he confessed, then quickly added, "but I don't want to be like my sister either."

"Of course you don't."

We then did a short survey of his strengths. Believe it or not, this kid was a leader. He didn't have any trouble getting kids to follow him. Being the first-born son, that didn't surprise me. The problem was, he used his leadership in such a way that people got hurt and laws got broken.

"You can still be a leader," I explained, "but now I want you to think first about where you want to take people. Do you want them to follow you to jail, or do you want to do something positive?"

91

Over the course of the next several weeks, we discussed and built on his other positive traits: people skills, creativity, and willingness to take risks (his first-born sister didn't have a risk-taking bone in her body). We began to develop a composite of how these same qualities could help him succeed in a positive way.

## The Family Den

If you were to visit me in my office and we started talking about birth order, I'd ask you to create a picture of your "family den." I'd want to know about mama bear, papa bear, oldest child bear, baby bear, and so on. The key, however, is not for me to understand your family but for you to understand your family.

Let me take you through this. I'll use a typical example. A woman (whom we'll call Andrea) comes into my office and tells me she is number three of four kids. She's six years younger than her older sister, seven years younger than her older brother, and two years older than her younger sister. Here's the profile skeleton:

Older brother: thirty-nine years old
Older sister: thirty-eight years old
Andrea: thirty-two years old
Younger sister: thirty years old

I begin by saying, "I want you to take a step back and look at the cubs that came out of your parents' den. Let's choose one word, an adjective, to describe each person's personality. What adjective would you use to describe your oldest sibling?"

"I guess I'd call him ambitious and a leader."

"I said *one* word."

"All right. A leader. But he really *was* ambitious. Today he's president of his own company."

"What about your big sister?"

"Oh, I don't know what's up with her. She's sort of the oddball maverick of the group. Cheryl has the least in common with anybody in our family. We're lucky if we hear from her at the holidays."

"Okay, we'll mark child number two down as the maverick, who rebelled against the whole family. Just as a curiosity point, is she well organized?"

"Heavens, no! We called her 'Pig Pen'."

"What about yourself?"

"That's what I don't understand. I read *The New Birth Order Book* and you kidded about your first-born wife being like Martha Stewart, and that's me. My husband laughed at me last week because we had company coming over in an hour and he caught me cleaning the top of the refrigerator. 'Andrea,' he said, 'Marty is only five feet eight, and his wife is shorter than that! The only way they're going to see the top of that refrigerator is with a ladder.' But I just can't help myself. If I'm the third born, how come I'm acting like a first born?"

"We'll get back to you, but for now let's move on to your youngest sister. Give me an adjective for her."

"She fits the mold, the classic princess who can do no wrong. I think she was my dad's favorite, although he never admitted it."

"What does she do today?"

"She's a mom, but she sells Mary Kay cosmetics on the side."

"A last born who is in sales? That's not too big of a shock! How does she do?"

"She's the best, which you can tell from five blocks away."

"What do you mean?"

"She has a bright pink Cadillac in the driveway. Of course, they give other options nowadays, but Missy has always been a show-off."

"All right, we'll call Missy the princess. Now, back to you: Why don't you understand yourself?"

"I'm so much like a first born, but I'm a third born. That just doesn't make any sense to me."

"Let's look at the big picture. Your oldest brother was what?"

"Really, really successful."

"And everybody looked up to him?"

"Yeah. Everybody went to him with their problems, including me. He was a really good brother."

"Can you see, though, that your older sister may have felt squeezed, like she couldn't compete with that older brother? And if life wasn't hard enough trying to compete with Mr. Superman, you come along and get everybody's attention. Now you're the mascot of the family. Everybody adores you. But at the same time, that six-year gap almost makes you the first born of the second family, doesn't it?"

"You know, it does. I guess I never thought of it that way, but I'm certainly Missy's big sister. Our other sister didn't want to have anything to do with her."

"Now the picture becomes a little clearer. Your older sister is taking on the role of the rebel. When you come along, someone has to step up to the plate and take on some responsibility—which you do. Now your youngest sister is born, and right above her is a feminine version of the superman big brother. So what does she become?"

"Irresponsible, with a capital *I*?"

"That's right, and do you understand why?"

"Because I was so responsible; is that what you're saying?"

"That's exactly what I'm saying. That's why the very things that make you get uptight seem to her like a fun challenge; that's why she drives a pink car and you drive a black minivan."

You can do the same thing—put a label on each of your siblings. Here are a few to consider, though I'm sure you can think of many others:

- Scholar
- Athlete
- Troublemaker
- Rebel
- Mom's favorite
- Dad's favorite
- Pushy
- Bossy
- Leader
- Miss Goody Two-shoes
- Little Miss Perfect
- Bully
- Clean freak
- Geek
- Computer whiz
- Loner
- Saint (very religious)
- Business titan
- Control freak
- Substitute mom (or substitute dad)
- Adventurer
- Poet
- Activist
- Comedian

The goal here is to gain a better understanding of how your siblings influenced your own role in life so that you can more objectively evaluate the personality you've developed in response and decide, as a mature adult, whether those traits are working for you.

## The Birth-Order Boost

In order to get a true boost out of your birth order, it's important to understand that birth order, by its nature, is based on the fluid dynamic relationship that exists between a parent and child as well as the children's reaction to one another. It's also important to remember that none of the birth orders are *better* than any other, they're just *different*. If you're a tricycle person, there's nothing wrong with that; just stay in the tricycle lane! Get out of the motorcycle lane, or else risk getting run over.

The bottom line, though—and I hope you understand this, because it's very important—is that every birth-order personality has something to offer. Even rebels have their place. In a sense, Nelson Mandela, Jesus, and Moses were all rebels. They challenged the status quo and worked to make a positive change. We need people who make us laugh, as well as meticulous people who can prepare our taxes. We need people to run for office and build successful companies, just as we need people who can resolve disputes and work through mediation. This world has a place for you, regardless of what title you think best fits your profile.

If you're a typical last born, getting an accountant's degree because that's what your older brothers did probably just isn't going to work for you. Those four walls will start to feel like a prison unless you can get out and breathe some social interaction. As a last born, you'll find that there are other occupations tailor-made for you.

As a middle child, ask yourself if you really want the pressures that come with being the top dog at work. Do you want to be the person whose decision will either run the company into the ground or finally make it financially profitable? Do you want to play the role of the bad guy who has to fire incompetent or lazy employees? If not, don't think that makes you less than a first born; it just means you need to find a different role to play at work.

If you're a first born, don't be surprised if last borns steal attention away from you or if middles seem to enjoy long, relational discussions while you are left a little out of the loop. Relational small talk probably isn't your bag—you'd try to start solving that person's problems inside of five minutes.

## At Peace with Your Parents

I've found birth order to be a major help in bringing about reconciliation within families. Once people realize a child's tendency is to go in the opposite direction of the sibling above him or her, parents and fellow siblings can have a bit more understanding. I'm not talking about making excuses, but it is helpful for moms and dads to know that following every saint, you're likely to raise an Attila the Hun.

You no longer have to guess why Timmy is so messy, why Ann is so bossy, why John is so religious, and why Tom always has to get his own way. It should no longer be a mystery to you why a sibling took off in the direction she did; based on birth order, that direction probably makes perfect sense.

When two siblings grew up fighting, it helps them gain a new appreciation for each other when I explain that their birth order and close proximity made them ideal candidates to go to war. As adults, they can look at this objectively and rebuild a new relationship in their later years.

I know what I'm talking about here. My two oldest daughters were born less than two years apart. They never stopped competing with each other—and in some ways, they are probably still competing. My two youngest daughters have a big space gap, and they have been two of the most cooperative sisters I've ever seen. While I'd like to take some credit for this—and I do believe Sande and I have improved our parenting over the years—the truth is, a lot of their relationship has to do with birth-order dynamics.

The same understanding can help parents and kids get along. There's a principle that rings pretty true: Most parents identify with their own birth order. If Mom is the baby, she'll naturally feel closest to the baby. If Dad is a middle child, he'll look out for the middle child, knowing firsthand how easy it is for middles to get neglected.

Don't feel left out by this. It doesn't mean your parents don't love you if you happen to be the first born and you've noticed that your dad has a soft spot for the baby; it's a naturally occurring phenomenon. Your dad is human; his reacting this way says absolutely nothing about your self-worth. Instead, it says everything about your dad's own history. Life is too short to take this personally.

The irony here, however, is that parents of the same birth order, while identifying with those children, also tend to butt heads with those children. A first-born dad and a first-born son likely will have some knock-down-drag-out scuffles. Hopefully fists will never fly, but boy, their strong wills and desire to control will create quite a few sparks.

What does all this mean? Give yourself and your family a heavy dose of grace. Break long-standing feuds. Reconcile with that difficult brother or sister. Consider giving that parent a second chance. Don't take natural slights personally. Sometimes something as simple as increased understanding can be the key to rebuilding strong family ties.

## In Pursuit of Maturity

It didn't take me long as a shrink to realize how many people were being impaled on an elusive pursuit of perfection. Few things are more destructive to us personally than perfectionism. Unfortunately, some people don't see perfectionism as a fault but as a goal. I've even had some Christians insist that the Bible calls us to be perfect. After all, in Matthew 5:48 Jesus says, "Be perfect, therefore, as your heavenly Father is perfect."

Well, I'm a Christian myself, and I have news for you—this verse doesn't call us to be perfect.

"How can you say that, Leman? How does 'be perfect' not mean 'be perfect'?"

Dr. Chuck Swindoll, a popular Christian author and president of Dallas Theological Seminary, helped me out with this one. The Greek word translated "perfect" is *teleios,* which really means "mature." Commentator David Hill points out, "The emphasis is not on flawless moral character, but on whole-hearted devotion to the imitation of God."[1]

*Teleios* speaks more of a mature approach to life and faith than it does of someone who never fails, never messes up, never says the wrong word, and never makes a mistake. If you're lost on your way toward perfection, let me give you a little hint: *You'll never get there.* The purpose of this book isn't to fix everything about you but to help you use several personality descriptors to point you in the right direction.

In other words, be the crummy, imperfect person you are and start serving now! You don't have to wait until you've got your act completely together (whatever that means) before you go back out into the world. Know your weaknesses and work on them. Become familiar with your strengths and make them even stronger. Understand your tendencies as a first born, middle, last born, or only, and bring a complementary circle of friends and people into your life that will help balance you out.

Now, having said all this, I need to add that you don't have all the information you need yet. From our study of the temperaments, hopefully you were able to get a handle on who you are. From our study of birth order, you should have been able to get a clearer picture of why you are the way you are. But there's another missing element: How have you individually responded to your temperament and birth order to create your own private logic? Why, for instance, are there last borns who are Democrats, last borns who are Republicans, and last borns who voted for Ralph Nader or Ross Perot, or who can't wait to vote for Arnold Schwarzenegger? Why do some first borns build big businesses and other first borns become social activists? Why do some middles become local judges while others become international diplomats? Why do some onlies succeed in athletics and others go to Hollywood?

We need to go a little deeper. We need to help you understand the early experiences that have shaped your worldview. To do that, we need to explore the powerful indicators of early childhood memories, which we'll turn our attention to in the next section.

# PART 3

# EARLY
# CHILDHOOD
# MEMORIES

# 6

# The Little Boy or Girl You Once Were, You Still Are

Step right up for the newest game show in town, *Who Wants to Be a Grown-Up?*

Guess what? You won the fastest-finger question and now sit in the hot seat. You've raced your way through all the piddly hundred-dollar questions, paused and used two of your lifelines to get through the bigger-dollar questions, and now you have just one question left to take home a million-dollar adult personality.

The studio lights are making you sweat. The makeup they put on your face is starting to streak. You take a desperate gulp of water and then almost choke on it as the host with the funny hair and the matching shirt and tie asks you the million-dollar question: "Describe for me three childhood memories."

"Wait a minute!" you protest. "This must be a trick question! What does being a grown-up have to do with childhood memories?"

"Is that your *final answer?*" the host asks you.

You think about it. You're pretty sure that the question is a trick; after all, the show is about maturity, and childhood memories are about when you were immature. But, hey, a million dollars is a lot of money. Maybe you should make sure.

"Uh, I'd like to use my last remaining lifeline. I'd like to phone a friend," you say.

"All right. Who would you like to phone?"

"Dr. Kevin Leman—he'll do."

Fortunately for you, I know the answer to that question. Early childhood memories have *everything* to do with becoming a mature adult. Answer the question!

If you truly want to understand why you act the way you do, you have one of two options: You can spend thousands of dollars to go to Aunt Moonwalker's five-day "Discover Yourself" workshop in the wilds of Montana, eating legumes and asparagus sandwiches while soaking in a volcanic-ash mudbath after walking across hot coals. *Or* you can stay in the comfort of your home and ask yourself the simple question, "What are my earliest childhood memories, and what do they say about me?"

As a therapist, I've found that few things unlock the secrets of a person's personality better than exploring the clues, private logic, and reminiscences of early childhood memories. In other words, to understand why you act the way you act as an adult, you need to go back to childhood.

Now I'm not saying that we can use past circumstances to avoid all personal responsibility: "My dad called me a sissy when I was eight, and that's why I became a bank robber." The fact is, while parental actions do affect us, they can affect us in very different ways. For instance, some women who are sexually abused become sexually promiscuous, while others shut down sexually and show no sexual interest at all—even toward their husbands.

Childhood memories aren't about *avoiding* responsibility, they're about *accepting* responsibility. They are tools we can use to determine what our deepest influences were so that we can address our tendencies (some good, some bad) as mature adults.

The basic principle behind childhood memories is this: The little boy or little girl you once were, you still are. Of course, you've lost some of the freckles and added a few moles. Your face has filled out and your hair might not be as thick or as blond. But in regard to your personality, your oldest memories are the major indicators of why you believe what you believe, why you do what you do, and why you behave the way you behave.

In fact, let me be so bold as to suggest that it's no accident why you hold on to certain memories and have seemingly forgotten others. Your brain is a very prejudiced tool; it holds on to what makes sense and discards what doesn't. If a memory of something that occurred two or three decades ago is still lodged in your mind, there's a reason for it, and the reason is this: Men and women remember only those events from early childhood that are consistent with their present view of themselves and the world around them.

Another phrase I use to describe this is your "private logic." Everybody has a private logic based on the real or imagined experiences they've had in their life, and out of this private logic they write their own unconscious rule book—their belief about how people should respond, and why. Some people feel they were picked on and that they always got a bad break, but that may not be true; it may just be the way they perceive their past. But that false perception is still affecting their personality and their view of the world.

Now that you know what I mean by memory, I should also define "early childhood." I'm talking about memories from eight years old and younger—second or third grade, for most of us. Why so young? Psychologists pretty much accept as a given that you've answered basic life questions and formed the basis of your personality by the age of five or six. Those central questions, "Who am I? What is my place in this world? How will I define good and evil? What is my purpose here?" will be answered ultimately by a private logic that you develop well before puberty.

As you mature, each decision you make and every situation you face is analyzed through this private logic. You justify your actions based on what you believe to be an objective system for understanding the world. When you go back to your early childhood, you're looking at less-filtered memories. In fact, you're probably thinking about the memories that *shaped* your current logic, rather than memories that have been clouded and reorganized by your current logic.

## Leman the Magician

Just for fun, let's try a little exercise here. This is really going to surprise some remaining skeptics. I want you to think of three early childhood memories and write them down on a piece of paper. Don't read any further until you finish this exercise. Close the book, write down your memories, and then come back. I'll wait for you.

Okay, some of you are cheating. Were you always like this? You're a little rebel, aren't you? You've kept reading without doing your homework, so I'm going to give you another chance. The surprise won't work if you skip this exercise! Go back and write down three of the first early childhood memories that come to mind.

All right—if you've made it this far, you're either obedient or very, very stubborn.

Let's say that you're a first-born choleric; let me take an educated guess at what you just wrote down. Of the three memories, one or all of the following will appear. You wrote down a hurtful time, a rule that you violated (or some memory about when you got into trouble), or a memory about achieving something. Or maybe you picked a memory that had great height or depth to it—there's movement: "I remember being on top of a roof and looking down at the ground," or "I remember looking up at my father," etc.

Now let's say you're a youngest born, a popular sanguine. You wrote down some happy memories: birthday parties, gifts you received, times when you were in the spotlight. If you wrote down surprises, they were probably positive surprises, when one of your needs was unexpectedly met. Your memories may also contain an "I'll show you" story— a time when someone said you couldn't do something, but that gave you motivation to go out and do it.

If you're a middle-born phlegmatic, you probably remember a time when somebody else got in a fight and ruined everything. You may have a few hard-luck stories about how you thought you were going to get a brand-new bike or coat and ended up with an older sibling's hand-me-down. It's very likely that your story will involve you as the negotiator, or perhaps a time when you were dominated and controlled and how angry that made you feel.

Am I right?

Ninety percent of the time, I will be.

Ask yourself: "How can a stranger who has never met me, talked to me, or even seen me, come so notoriously close to pinning down my early childhood memories?" The answer is simple: You remember the things that are consistent with your private logic. Since I've counseled hundreds of first borns and just as many last borns, not to mention middles, I know exactly what most of you are thinking.

While I was finishing this book, I was at the Christian Booksellers Association annual convention—a weeklong whirl of book publicity for publishers, editors, salespeople, and, oh yeah, writers. I've been going to these meetings for years, and while going to this event was a bit intoxicating as a new author, after just a few years it became more than a little tiresome having a full day of signing books, giving interviews, and meeting with publishers.

When I'm feeling a bit bored or tired, I always know where to bail out. I can usually spot the groups of sales guys without too much trouble, so I'll pull up a chair and ask, "Can I join you?"

That's where it gets fun.

One guy was being polite and asked me what my next book project was going to be. "I'm writing a book on why you are the way you are, helping people to understand their personality."

"How are you going to do that?"

"Well, for instance, I'll take them through their early childhood memories."

He kind of scoffed. "I don't know if I believe in that early childhood memory stuff."

I could tell by his cynical, analytical nature and his impeccable dress that I was talking to a first born, so I decided to have a little fun.

"Well, you know, they're pretty powerful indicators," I offered. "In fact, why don't you give me an early childhood memory of yours?"

But then I stopped myself and added, "Better yet, let *me* give you your early childhood memories."

This guy looked at me like I was absolutely nuts.

I turned a card over and wrote down three general memories: achievement; breaking a rule; and depth, movement, or height.

"All right," I said. "Think about three childhood memories, and then describe the first one for me. They need to be before you turned eight years old."

"Well, I remember being on my grandfather's farm, sitting on top of a hayloft, looking out from there."

I said, "Bingo," and pointed to what I had written on the card. His jaw dropped open in astonishment. He looked further up my list, and then he was really surprised. "Hey," he said, "you got my second memory too!" He then talked about breaking one of his grandfather's rules.

The reason I was able to do this is because birth order and memories are usually pretty closely aligned. If I know someone's birth order, I can usually predict the general nature of their memories. When I appeared on a show in Dallas, I invited callers to phone in and give me their early childhood memories. After hearing their memories, I told them their birth order. The callers and the host were amazed, but in all honesty, there's not that much to it. In fact, once you're done with this book, you should be able to do the same thing.

While the fact that our memories can be conditioned by our birth order may be troubling to some, it can be absolutely exhilarating to others: "You mean, I've *learned* to become the person I am?"

Yes! You are the way you are because of the choices you have made in response to your surrounding environment.

So what's the good news? The good news is this: If you're a flaw-picking, cynical, and abrasive person who is eating up more friends than you can replace, with God's help you can change. If you're a happy-go-lucky kind of person but totally ditzy and even irresponsible, you can develop the necessary good qualities to balance your adorable absent-mindedness. Once you understand what makes you tick, you can forge new patterns of behavior and remake your personality.

109

## But I Don't Have Any Memories

Talking about early childhood memories usually gets a room buzzing, but there are always a few who stand up and insist, "But, Dr. Leman, I don't have any childhood memories."

Yes, you do. Though many of us wish we could push "rewind," or even better, "delete," in our brains, the fact is, we can't. What you have done, seen, experienced, and felt is recorded in the deep recesses of your mind. Just because you have a hard time getting at the memories doesn't mean they aren't in there.

There is one exception, of course: In the case of severe trauma—gross abuse or overwhelming tragedy—the brain does sometimes call into play a very effective coping mechanism that we counselors call "denial." Denial has its place—it allows kids to put off dealing with traumatic events until they reach their late twenties or early thirties (typically), when they will have the maturity to finally face the truth. I hope you realize that this book is not intended to replace professional counseling—if you've had this kind of experience in the past, you need to see a trained therapist. But for the rest of you, I'd like to provide a few moves to help you restore memories that have seemingly been sent to the recycle bin in your mind.

### Relax

Bringing up memories is most effectively done with a quiet mind. The reason some people blot out their childhood is that they are so busy today they just can't slow down. They're so used to operating at maximum capacity that something about taking a time-out feels wrong. Find a quiet place, turn off the TV, and do some introspective thinking.

110

*Provoke Your Memories*

Ask yourself some of these questions:

- What is your earliest school-related memory? Can you think of a teacher you liked (or disliked), a classmate who was a close friend, or a bully who mistreated you?
- Do you have any memories of doing something alone with one of your parents?
- How did your family spend holidays? Is there a particularly painful (or happy) birthday or Christmas memory lurking in there?
- Did you have any pets growing up? Do you remember ever turning to your pet for solace or to talk out a problem?
- What was your neighborhood like? Think about some of the families who lived near you. Anything come to mind?
- How did your family spend its leisure time? Do you recall any summer vacations or special weekend outings?
- Where did you sit at the table? What was mealtime like at your home? Did you even have mealtimes together?
- Describe your early childhood bedroom. What was on the walls? What did you keep near your bed? Did you ever hide anything in your bedroom?
- Who taught you how to swim? How to ride a bike? How to catch a baseball?
- Who talked to you about God, faith, and religion? Did your family attend religious services? If so, what were they like? Was there a big difference between how your parents acted at church or synagogue and how they acted at home?

111

- How were you disciplined?
- Do thoughts of your childhood room make you feel comforted, sad, lonely, or scared?

### Talk to Your Siblings

Sometimes talking over past vacations, holidays, and family stories with other siblings can do wonders to release your own memories. Be careful here, however. Sometimes family stories can take on the nature of legends, and truth can get rewritten. Make sure the memory is *your* memory and make sure it really happened. Use your siblings more as people who can help provoke your memories than as people who can fill in the details.

Perhaps even more helpful than talking to your siblings is going through old photographs or home movies. A picture of a lamp, a teddy bear, or an old outfit can release any number of early childhood memories.

### Get Specific

General memories won't work for this exercise. "I always liked to ride my bike after school" isn't a memory; it's a generalization. A memory has to refer to a specific event that occurred at a specific time, even if you can't place the exact date: "One time when I was riding my bike after school, I crashed into the family station wagon and got into trouble." That's a memory! Keep reaching for specific events.

## Warning! Memories Can Lie like Dogs

I suppose that just about everybody older than thirty has heard of Joe DiMaggio, one of baseball's all-time greatest players. What you may not know is that DiMaggio had a younger brother named Dom who was nearly as good a player—and some say an even better fielder. Casey Stengel once said, "With the possible exception of his brother Dom, Joe is the best outfielder in the league."[1]

While Dom was excellent in the outfield and an accomplished hitter, he could never quite match his older brother's dominance at the plate. No one could. In 1941 Joe made history as he tied Willie Keeler's record for consecutive games with a hit (forty-four). DiMaggio needed just one more game to break the record and have it all to himself.

As fate would have it, game forty-five was played against the Boston Red Sox—Dom's team. Dom often told the story of being out in the field when a long line drive leapt off Joe's bat in the first inning. Dom recalls making a leaping catch and depriving Joe of a hit, which he says was like driving a stake through Joe's heart.

"As we crossed paths in the outfield, I tried to avoid making eye contact with him, but he was staring me down," Dom recalls. "If looks could kill, I would have dropped dead on the spot."[2]

This incident says a lot about sibling rivalry, younger brother–older brother relations, and Dom's personality in particular. There's just one problem with this story, however. Dom DiMaggio didn't make that catch—Stan Spence did. Look it up in the record books; it's right there. But you couldn't convince Dom that he wasn't the one who put his brother's streak in jeopardy more than sixty years ago. (For all you baseball buffs, Joe grounded out in his second at bat but homered in his third to keep the streak alive, which eventually ended at fifty-six.)

Memories are by no means infallible. In fact, they lie like dogs. Years ago, my good friend Moonhead and I were in midget league baseball (not to be confused with Little League, which hadn't been invented yet—which just goes to show how old I am). Moonhead and I have been friends since we were both three years old, and every year we have

113

an annual fight over the "fact" that as manager of our base-ball team, he didn't give me a hat. We didn't have full uniforms back in those days, but we did get a shirt and a cap, and Moonhead's job was to make sure I got mine. But since I missed a couple practices (when my family went on the only family vacation we ever had), Moonhead said I wouldn't get a hat.

To be fair, Moonhead disputes my story. He insists that he gave me a hat and I probably lost it. But I am just as convinced that he is lying. It's been forty-seven years, and stubborn old Moonhead still won't admit he's wrong.

"Leman," he says, "you know me; I'm not a petty guy. It isn't my nature to do something like that."

"Oh, yeah?" I say. "Sounds to me like a classic case of denial. The truth is too painful for you to admit. Look at this!" I took out my trump card, an old team picture that clearly shows me as the only player with a different cap.

"That doesn't prove anything," Moonhead says. "You're a last born. You were losing things all the time."

"It does too prove something," I counter. "It proves you punished me for nothing and made me go an entire season wearing a different-colored hat."

"Leman, you get things in your head. What do you psychologists call it? Transposition or something like that?"

What strikes me about this annual argument (except for the fact that Moonhead still won't admit he's wrong) is that two grown men can be so adamant about something that happened so long ago. Both of us are absolutely, positively convinced that we are right, but there's just one thing for certain: Only one of us is right. The other one is lying.

Me, Moonhead, and Dom DiMaggio show how easily we can manufacture and edit our memories, particularly those from our childhood. A study recently released in the *Journal of Experimental Psychology* found that "people unconsciously tamper with their own memories, inventing causes for events they see around them to help make sense of things."[3] For example, a study in *Psychology and Marketing* found that 35 percent claimed to have shaken hands with Bugs Bunny on a past visit to the Magic Kingdom.[4] Of course, Bugs Bunny is a Warner Brothers creation, not a Disney character. No child has ever shaken Bugs's hand inside the happiest place on earth, even though a lot of people "remember" doing so.

Mark Reinitz, a psychologist at the University of Puget Sound in Tacoma, Washington, explains, "Memory isn't a record. It's an interpretation to a large extent."[5] This doesn't discount our childhood memories. In fact, in one sense, it provides all the more reason to analyze them. A false memory may yield even more understanding than a true one. Psychologist Elizabeth Loftus says, "Memory is malleable for a reason. It helps us remember ourselves in a more positive light."[6]

The important thing is for you to look at your memories objectively to understand the personal logic by which you approach life. Once you've begun building a pool of memories, you can begin analyzing them to help you understand your assumed rule book. To help you in this exercise, allow me to share one or two memories of my own.

## The Wayward Cub

I grew up with the nickname "Cub," or "Cubby." My father gave this name to me when I was just eleven days old. He picked me up in his hands, chuckled, and said, "This boy looks just like a little bear cub."

Of course, I have no memory of my dad doing that, but being called "Cubby" shaped me in many ways. As I stated earlier, any name with a *y* ending—Bobby, Jimmy, Annie, Suzy—usually indicates last-born status. A first born would normally change his or her name to Bob, Jim, Ann,

115

or Susan. Being called by a kid-sounding name affects how you view yourself.

That's why some memories stick in a very vivid way. One memory I don't expect I'll ever forget occurred when I was in Cub Scouts as a young boy. During one den meeting, that week's den mother brought out some of her famous peanut butter cookies.

Unfortunately, she served them on a very expensive china plate.

As a young kid, if I ate lunch at noon, I'd be hungry again by 1:30 or 2:00. It was well into the afternoon, and I smelled those cookies before I saw them. When she placed the cookies on the edge of the table, one cookie in particular caught my eye. Bigger than the rest, with just the right amount of sugar sprinkled on top, it practically had my name written on it.

The challenge, of course, was that there were six or seven other grubby little scouts who saw the plate the same time I did. That plate had barely touched the table when my hand went out to grab the prized cookie. Tragically my enthusiasm got the better of me, and my elbow sent the plate flying. It was the worst three seconds of my life, watching that china plate take off from the table and go hurtling toward its demise on the hard floor below.

There was a crash, a gasp, and then a terrible scolding: "Cubby Leman! Every time you walk into this house something gets broken!"

To make matters worse, the plate turned out to be an heirloom—it had belonged to my den mother's great-grandmother and could never be replaced. Her words weren't unkind, nor were they unfair. Looking back as an adult, I can understand why she would lash out after losing something with such sentimental value. Even as a kid, I knew she was right; there were any number of mothers who could have said the same thing: "Cubby Leman! Every time you walk into this house something gets broken!"

116

Eventually I got thrown out of scouts. The final straw came the day our den had planned a big tour that required a minimum number of participants. I had signed up to attend, but something happened that morning and I decided not to go. That's a typical last-born trait, by the way—it wasn't convenient, so I blew it off.

Well, as it turned out, my not showing up meant that nobody could participate, because without me they didn't have enough people. The whole den lost out. If I had called and canceled, the den master at least could have notified everybody before they showed up. My lack of common courtesy made everybody lose half a day, and the scout leader had had enough. I was gone.

Another memory has a similar theme. My mom used to subject our Christmas tree to what I thought were ugly antique Norwegian ornaments she had inherited from my grandmother. What's worse, Mom wouldn't let me get the nice shiny bulbs from the dime store because our tree was too full of those ugly antique ones, so I did what any enterprising young boy would do. I took out my pellet gun and had target practice.

You should have seen those ornaments burst apart! I had never seen anything like it. There was a very satisfying "pop" when they were hit and then the coolest shatter you've ever seen. Before I knew it, I had just about cleared the tree.

As I looked on my work with satisfaction, it suddenly dawned on me that I was looking at quite a mess and that my mom, who didn't share my opinion on the aesthetic value of these bulbs, might be less than pleased with someone for shooting them up.

(Do I hear some readers saying, "Leman, I'm glad you're not my kid!")

I gathered up my gun and fled the scene. About twenty minutes later, I heard a shriek and ran into the living room. "What is it, Mom?" I asked, looking horrified, shocked, and amazed that such a thing could have happened in the peaceful Leman abode.

"Cubby!" my mom started to yell. "Did you do this?"

"Wasn't me, Mom," I lied. "Must have been the cat."

Mom bought my explanation, and the cat paid a heavy price. I remember my mom being pretty easy to fool. I get a kick out of hearing people ask her about me today. "Oh, he was always such a *good* boy," she'll say, only because she never knew the half of it.

What do these memories mean? As I've already stated, you remember things that are consistent with how you view life. If I were counseling myself, I'd say, "Kevin, you see yourself as a rule breaker, a rebel, don't you?"

I certainly do. One of my more common thoughts growing up was "Oh, crud, I'm in trouble again." I was always in trouble for *something*. Consequently, rules don't mean that much to me—even today. I've broken rules all my life. For instance, in the academic world, there's an unwritten law that you're not supposed to do all your studies at the same school. You're supposed to get your bachelor's degree at one school, go to a different school for your master's degree, and then go to yet a third school for your doctorate. Occasionally you'll see people get their master's and doctorate at the same place, but not that often. To get all three degrees from the same institution, however, is unheard of.

Except that I did it. I liked the University of Arizona, and I didn't want to go anywhere else—so I didn't!

I continue my quest to break the rules. More than a few passengers have turned their heads my way when I've boarded an airplane in the dead of winter wearing shorts. Can I help it if the rest of the country doesn't have the good sense to move to Tucson when it gets cold everywhere else?

Legalists who live only by rules, many of which are made up by humans, have always driven me up the wall.

My faith is very important to me. Being faithful to my wife and family is near the top of my list. But following rules for rules' sake—you don't chew gum in church, you only watch movies with G ratings, you don't speak about certain subjects (that is, my favorite subject, sex!)—I have almost no tolerance for that line of thinking.

In fact, I've had more than one editor who got a little offended by my early manuscripts. Some writers I know would be mortified if an editor wrote them a note saying they were offended by something they had just read. Me? I take it as a badge of honor. If what I write doesn't upset a few people—especially a few Christians—I don't feel like I've done my job. What else is a book or a talk supposed to do if not rock the boat a little? If everybody agrees with everything I say, why am I wasting my time saying it?

Do you see how the memory shapes who I am as an adult? I'm no longer breaking plates (well, occasionally), but the mind-set is still there.

Breaking rules doesn't scare me. Having the label of a rebel really doesn't bug me. Even more important, I'm comfortable with it. I use it to my advantage. I see it as one of the unique things that makes me who I am. Instead of running from it, I try to capitalize on it and put it to good use.

On the other hand, I use this part of my rule book to caution myself not to go too far. It's one thing to oppose religious legalists; it's another thing entirely to do something that is truly immoral. When I'm speaking to certain audiences, I don't mind pushing the envelope, but I try very hard not to bust it open either. I want to respect and honor the people who invited me.

By analyzing all of this, I'm able to use and shape my rule book instead of allowing it to run my life. Since I've talked so much about this rule book, perhaps we need to spend some time defining and discussing it. We'll do this in the next chapter.

# 7

# Your Rule Book

ne person drives his car directly into the Employee of the Month parking space even though he's not an employee and there's an empty stall right next to it, while another person passes up the space even though doing so means walking one hundred yards in the rain.

Why?

One college grad sends out fifty resumes and doesn't get a single request for an interview, so she follows up each "silent" response with a personal visit to the company and ends up getting five job offers. Another woman sends out three resumes, receives three rejections, and quits looking, taking an entry-level job with her father's company instead—even though she has a four-year degree and is seriously overqualified for the position.

Why?

One father takes a very laid-back approach to parenting. His grade school kids go to bed only when they get tired, even if that means staying up until ten or eleven at night, and they all have permission to eat whenever they want to as long as they clean up their mess. Another dad treats bedtime like a divine mandate. If his eight-year-old isn't in bed by 8:30, she'll be grounded the next day after school. And once dinner is over, there is absolutely no way any food is going into her mouth until breakfast is served the next morning.

Why?

In each scenario, the people are acting according to rule books that make sense to them. One rule book says, "The day is more fun when you bend the rules; life is too short to let other people tell you what to do." These people enjoy getting others upset by deliberately flaunting their independence. They park in areas where they're not supposed to park, they say things that might shock others, and they sometimes dress in a way that is sure to garner attention.

Another group lives by the motto "If I break a rule—any rule—the punishment will be severe and far greater than any enjoyment I might get out of doing what I want. Therefore, I won't break any rule, no matter what." Such a person is likely to be unusually submissive, the kind that producers have great fun with on *Candid Camera.* They'll do anything you ask them to if they sense you have the authority to ask them to do it. Simply put up a sign and they'll obey it.

In the example about two college graduates, the first woman is living by a rule book that says, "I always find a way; when people tell me I can't do something, that just makes me want to prove them wrong." Under this guideline for living, rejection doesn't act as a deterrent—it's a stimulus. It gets her motivated. Another person has a rule book that says, "Every time I stick my neck out, it gets cut off. It hurts more to be rejected than anything else, so I'm not going to try anymore." A person who believes this to be true will give up at the first sign of struggle and settle in at Daddy's company without really trying to prove her worth in the outside world.

These rule books are shaped by our response to our childhood memories, our upbringing, and our birth order. Rule books within families will usually have some similarities, but they will also have marked differences. Ultimately your rule book is a very individual thing, and it governs virtually everything you do.

## Titanic Tendencies

My goal in this section is to help you critique your own worst critic—that ever-present rule book. We do this by understanding tendencies that come from early childhood memories.

I hope you've taken the time to write down your three memories. If you *still* haven't, may I ask you once again to pause for five minutes and do so? This chapter will be much more beneficial if you take the time to do this.

Once you have your three memories, I'm going to ask you to evaluate them in a couple different ways. First, we'll use the memories to explore what kind of parents you had, and then we'll use the memories to understand your temperament.

### Memories of Authoritarian Parents

If your parents were unduly harsh and subscribed to the lay-down-the-law-and-take-no-prisoners approach to parenting, you probably have memories that have you getting in trouble for breaking the rules. Because there were so many rules, it might have felt like you were *always* breaking at least one of them.

One of my clients, "Mark," grew up with very strict religious parents. He wasn't allowed to shop on Sundays. He didn't understand why; his parents had mentioned something about a Sabbath, but he didn't know what that really meant.

On one hot summer Sunday, Mark's best buddy rode his bike up to Mark's house, peddling as if his life were in danger.

"What's up?" Mark asked.

"They just got Brooks Robinson's cup in at the 7–Eleven!" the buddy responded.

Mark was a die-hard Orioles fan, and the 7–Eleven had pictures of major league baseball players on their plastic cups that year. My client couldn't wait to get a cup with his favorite third baseman on it.

He ran into the house to get his money when his mom asked him what the hurry was. All of a sudden, Mark remembered it was Sunday and his mom wouldn't appreciate his spending money at a store, not even a 7–Eleven.

"Uh, Jimmy just captured a snake at his house. I'm going over to see it."

"Okay, but be back by 5:00. We're eating an early dinner tonight."

Mark jumped on his bike and rode with Jimmy to the 7–Eleven. He could taste that cherry slurpee even before he touched it. The cool drink felt good in his hand, and boy, what a thrill to see Brooks Robinson's picture and a stamped autograph on the cup! Just as Mark and Jimmy walked out of the convenience store, Mark's next-door neighbors—members of his family's church—walked by.

"Why, Mark, what are you doing here on a Sunday?"

Suddenly that cold slurpee felt like a death warrant. There was no way Mark could hide the evidence in his hand, and he knew without asking that the first thing these neighbors would do when they got home would be to talk to his parents. He dropped that slurpee into the trash and sadly walked his bike home.

While this story tugs at the heartstrings, what's most significant to me as a psychologist is the fact that a man in his late thirties is still haunted by this memory. Both of Mark's parents have died—but their style of parenting is still very much with him.

Authoritarian parents also have a tendency to withhold emotional warmth and involvement. One client shared a telling story with me. When she was six years old, she drew a picture for her mother. She had overheard her mother say how much she enjoyed a good sunset, so her daughter worked the better part of two days on drawing just such a scene. Finally, when she thought she had it just right, she proudly showed it to her mom, who was busy cleaning the kitchen and who seemed to resent the interruption. Mom said, "That's nice, dear," and immediately put the picture down. The girl was hurt beyond words, but not nearly as much as she was two days later when she was putting out the trash and found the picture crumpled up in the garbage can.

Now I'm guessing your heart goes out to this little girl, but keep in mind, the woman telling it to me was in her forties. What's so significant about this story is not that a little girl had her heart broken by her mom but that a forty-one-year-old woman still remembered it happening to her and felt the pain as if she were still six years old. That tells you something.

If you had very authoritarian parents, it's likely that you're going to display some of the following personality characteristics. Keep in mind, some of these traits contradict each other—we all respond differently when facing the same type of pressure—but these are the most typical responses to overly strict parenting.

- You'll wait until your teenage or college years to rebel and then flaunt your independence in the face of virtually any authority.
- You'll become extremely compliant, quiet, and cooperative on the outside—but you'll also be very timid and shy internally.
- You'll go out of your way to be obnoxious; you'll start stupid quarrels, get into lots of fights, and be very rude and abrasive.
- You'll lack the ability to be spontaneous and to be an independent thinker. You'll have very little creativity; instead, you'll see everything in black and white.
- You'll rely on other people to make decisions for you. Internally you'll feel like you need to be controlled, like you have to have some authority directly over you. Otherwise life is too scary.

### Memories of Lenient Parents

Even as a seven-year-old, Doug knew he could do no wrong. His parents never held him accountable, and they even frequently went out of their way to defend him. Doug loved it at first. He knew he could get away with anything. That's why he thought he'd help himself out at the local junior fishing derby. After he pulled a bass out of the lake, he dropped a bunch of sinkers down its throat to increase the weight.

The judges weren't naïve. They had seen every trick invented and then some. They quickly discovered the sinkers and disqualified the boy's entry.

The father was furious—but at the judges, not at Doug. He thought they should just pour out the sinkers and weigh the empty fish. His son had made an error in judgment, but why disqualify him for a childish mistake that probably every kid had tried at least once?

I recently read of a classic case of a very lenient parent. John Daly is well known in the golf world as a troubled soul. Though he had some remarkable early successes on the professional golf tour, he has had even more struggles. To begin with, he has an ongoing problem with his weight. One of his favorite breakfasts is biscuits with chocolate gravy. His desire for alcohol is so strong that he once drove away from a rehab unit, knowing that doing so would cost him a $3-million-a-year endorsement contract with Callaway Golf. He has run up over $2 million in gambling debts and has been divorced twice—even though he's just thirty-five years old. To help tame his volcanic temper, which has led to his arrest for domestic disturbance on several occasions, doctors have put him on just about every manic-depressive drug imaginable: Lithium, Prozac, Xanax, Paxil. You name it, he's been on it.[1]

I could go on and on, but I think you get the point. This is a troubled young man. Yet when John Daly's dad was interviewed, he couldn't understand why Daly's sponsors made such a fuss. "And they're controllin' [his] life! Here's a guy who really doesn't have any problems, except that he likes to drink. . . . OK, John had a few drinks and hit some golf balls maybe where he shouldn't. Because of that, they put him in rehab?"[2]

Look, any man who has several arrests for domestic disturbance, is running up million-dollar gambling debts, and has twice called friends threatening to commit suicide certainly has a few problems—more than just "liking to drink." But some parents just can't see the trouble their kids are really getting into—and they remain lenient to their dying day, much to their child's harm.

If your parents were too lenient, I bet you have memories of getting away with something but maybe feeling a little guilty about it afterward. Your memories probably also center around getting presents, having parties, taking trips, being absolutely spoiled at Christmas, and indulging in other activities. While such parenting might allow you to have what you think is a little extra fun as a kid, it can reap disastrous results for your personality as an adult.

If your parents were too lenient, your rule book probably contains some of the following:

- You have a tendency to be extremely self-centered; because you always got your own way, you have what others see as an amazing lack of empathy and consideration for others.
- You come off as socially adept, but you lack the internal ability to truly care about others and develop deep relationships. Therefore, most of your friends are casual friends who know they can't count on you.
- If you see something you want, you do your best to get it, regardless of what it costs or what the consequences of your actions may be.
- You have a judgmental spirit and a critical tongue.
- You've probably picked up at least one addiction. It might be gambling, overeating, sex, or drinking, but in one area you show little or no restraint.

### Memories of Critical Parents

One of the sadder cases I've worked on concerned a family with an overly critical dad. His son Bobby was a pretty good ballplayer. He wasn't the best hitter on the team, but he did bat leadoff, which meant the coach saw him as one of the most reliable and consistent batters to get on base. The boy's dad never got around to watching any of his son's games. He worked long hours and demanded as much from himself as he did from his kids. But after Bobby begged all spring, his dad finally agreed to leave work early (6:00 P.M.) and make it to his son's game.

"Will you make me proud, Son?" the dad asked that morning.

"I will, Dad," Bobby replied.

There was something in the dad's question that unleashed any number of negative emotions in the boy. The question was really more a command: "Don't embarrass me, don't let me down, don't make me look like a fool." The dad obviously had his own insecurity problems, and these problems were leaking into his parenting.

The boy became very nervous as the day wore on. He was excited that his dad would finally see him play, but he was getting more anxious by the hour. After all, the very best hitters in Little League scarcely batted more than .400; just what was his dad expecting him to do? How would his dad react to a strikeout?

Finally, 6:00 P.M. arrived. As the leadoff hitter, Bobby was the very first batter in the game. He looked at his dad just before he got to the plate and felt his stomach flip-flop. There was no word of encouragement; rather, he received a warning glare, and every negative phrase he had heard growing up came hurtling back into this young man's mind. He barely knew which end of the bat to hold by the time he reached the plate.

The first pitch hit the dirt in front of the plate. To the coach's astonishment, his leadoff hitter swung at—and of course missed—this terrible pitch. The next pitch was high, almost over the batter's head. Again, Bobby swung. Again, the entire crowd groaned.

The boy, in a panic now, tried to gather his strength.

"All right now, Bobby," the coach called out. "Make him pitch to you."

Bobby nodded and stepped back into the box. *Don't swing at just anything,* he told himself, terrified that he would strike out.

That's why he left the bat on his shoulder as the pitcher delivered a fastball right down the middle of the plate, a pitch that Bobby normally would have sent careening into center field.

"Strike three, you're ouuuuttt!" the umpire yelled.

Three pitches. Three strikes.

Bobby turned fearfully toward the stands, only to see his dad's back as he walked away. Bobby's dad wasn't going to stay if his son was going to embarrass him.

Adults who had critical parents often report memories in which they are laughed at for making a simple, childish mistake—misspelling an easy word or incorrectly answering a rather simple math formula.

If your parents were too critical, I bet you can relate to some of the following:

- You often procrastinate, making the excuse that there's not enough time, but in truth you're simply afraid to have anything you do evaluated.
- You carry a lot of guilt and negative self-speak. You criticize yourself mercilessly for the smallest mistake, and you have a hard time forgetting any instance where you've let yourself or someone else down.
- You never believe that you truly measure up; you always feel like you're letting someone down, that you could be doing it just a little bit better. Even when others praise your work, you think they're just being nice to you.
- You have very little self-confidence and almost no self-esteem.
- You don't picture yourself as a success; even if you stumble onto financial or vocational success, you always expect the "other shoe to drop." You're just waiting for the bottom to fall out and be exposed as the loser you know you are.

## Your Bent

We've looked at your memories in relation to how your parents treated you. Now let's look at memories that reveal your own tendencies. Your parents' style of child rearing has certainly shaped you, but you also made some choices about how you would respond. In addition to understanding how you were raised, you need to get a feel for what traits you developed in response.

Keep in mind, none of these categories we're about to discuss are necessarily bad. For instance, even being a controller can be a good trait. I know a lot of nurses who are wonderful controllers, and I'm glad they take charge.

Instead of seeing a label as bad or good, the important thing is to get a better understanding of your own disposition. You've examined your parents, and now you can examine yourself.

The most common categories of memories include the controller, the pleaser, the charmer, and the victim.

### The Controller

A controlling memory is one in which you're in charge—you're arranging the neighborhood game, you're the kid called on in the case of an emergency, you're bringing order to chaos. Controlling memories are particularly common with choleric temperaments.

If I notice controlling early childhood memories in your past, I can make some basic assumptions about who you are. It's likely that you place high expectations on yourself and on others. You may prefer to work alone because then nobody can mess up what you're doing. You probably hate surprises because you never want to be caught off guard or ill prepared. You draw great satisfaction from accomplishing something, are probably

131

pretty competitive, and prefer to be the person in charge. In your view, people tend to be a little too laid-back—if they don't want to win, they shouldn't play the game. I wouldn't be surprised if you have a little problem with your temper.

I worked with a choleric temperament (a first born, naturally) who had controlling early childhood memories. He was a classic textbook choleric in many regards. His wife made a terrible mistake for his forty-fifth birthday party—she decided to surprise him. Had she consulted me, I would have told her a surprise party is the last thing she should have considered, but as a sanguine she thought a surprise birthday party would be fun.

Strike one.

Because the wife had to prepare the rented hall for the birthday, she arranged to have her teenage son convince his dad that he needed a ride to the hall for a church youth group function. Well, the wife didn't realize that her choleric husband had plans for the day—he was finally going to get the fence stained.

When the son went outside to request a ride, his dad was wearing an old paint shirt, colorful outdated shorts, scummy tennis shoes, and a paint hat. The son suggested that maybe the dad would like to change, but the dad looked at his son like he was crazy: "Why do I need to change to give you a lift to the Grange Hall?"

The son was faced with a dilemma—either spoil the surprise or let his dad drive him to the party wearing that ridiculous outfit. The boy decided to maintain the surprise and let his dad come dressed as he was.

Strike two.

Dad showed up looking ridiculous, and the son convinced him that he needed to walk into the hall. By that time, the dad was suspicious. When he realized his friends and family members were waiting to yell, "Surprise!" he was far more agitated than he was pleased. He hated being put in a situation for which he wasn't dressed appropriately. Besides, he had left the stain and paint brushes out, and all he could think about was the half-finished project he left at home.

Strike three.

If you're a choleric first born with controlling memories, have a frank talk with your family. Explain how you like things to be run. Give them a chance to understand you and to avoid making mistakes that would seem obvious to you but that may not seem obvious to them.

### The Pleaser

Pleaser memories are most common among women. I've known a few men with pleaser memories, but this is one category that is definitely gender biased. Maybe a little girl tried to help her dad by painting the house, but she made a mess of it. Perhaps she tried to help him shine his shoes, and she missed a spot. Or maybe she even attempted to mow the lawn and ran over some flowers by mistake. Other pleaser memories end with the child taking blame— whether or not he or she was actually at fault.

I see pleaser memories most often with phlegmatic middle borns and compliant first borns. Usually these people lack confidence, live with a good bit of fear (always waiting for the other shoe to drop), let people run over them, rarely stand up for themselves, and have generally low self-esteem.

If you're a phlegmatic pleaser, you're a sucker for any loser who happens to cross your path. You'll be able to convince yourself that this guy has always been misunderstood, and if someone would just love him, he'd reform himself. Most likely the loser you hook up with is a strong controller, and he'll play you like a Stradivarius. He knows just what buttons to push and how to manipulate your emotions so that you'll spare no amount of money, time, or energy on him.

One of your greatest weaknesses is basing your sense of self-worth solely on your performance. You need to learn how to stand up for yourself, how to say no, and how to take charge of your own life. You're not important only for what you do—you matter for who you are. But this will be one of the most difficult lessons for you to learn.

## The Charmer

You can probably tell by now that sanguines and last borns will usually have charmer-related memories. Charmers recall times when they made the entire family laugh or when they manipulated their parents, schoolteachers, or siblings to get their own way. Memories in which you are the center of attention also qualify as charmer-related.

Here's a common charmer memory: "I was five years old, very small for my age, and the last of the grandchildren. One day when we were all gathering at my aunt's house for Thanksgiving, Grandma and Grandpa walked into the dining room, and Grandpa went straight to me, lifted me up, and said, 'Missy, how I've missed you!' He gave me a big kiss and a hug and made me promise that I'd never grow up. Then Grandma said, 'Herbert, don't forget to say hi to the other children. They're waiting for you too.' It made me feel really special that Grandpa paid the most attention to me."

If you have charmer memories, you probably enjoy the spotlight. You feel most alive when you've made a room laugh, and you feel most depressed when you think you're being ignored or treated as insignificant. You're probably an extrovert and very likely have a tendency to pout when you don't get your own way.

*The Victim*

Do your memories leave you feeling like you got a raw deal? Do they dredge up feelings of injustice and perhaps resentment?

If so, you may qualify as a victim.

Victims are usually middle children. They believe that if something goes wrong, they are the ones most likely to be blamed—because they often have been! Here's a classic victim memory shared by a former client:

"I was six years old. There was a group of about eight children—including two of my siblings—playing kickball in our front yard. One kid kicked the ball into the road, and a neighbor boy ran out to retrieve it. He didn't look where he was going and ran right in front of a car. The driver slammed on his brakes and missed the kid. We all ran out to the street to see what had happened and were followed closely by my mom. She was so scared and angry and, because I was holding the ball, assumed I had caused the problem. She spanked me in front of everyone, even though some of the other kids were yelling, 'He didn't do it.' What bugged me most was that she assumed it was me. I was always getting the blame."

As a victim, you consider yourself one of the most unlucky people in the world. You may feel most comfortable when others show you pity. You might be slightly paranoid and eventually develop ailments (such as excessive weight gain or a never-ending list of medical ailments) that fit right in line with how you see yourself. Both of these conditions keep getting you noticed, but eventually you're going to have to learn that's not the best way to be noticed.

These roles have shaped your interactions with others. The controller wants respect; the charmer wants affection; the victim wants pity; the pleaser wants to be appreciated.

People pick this up. Sometimes I can have a first-time client walk into my office and within five seconds I know exactly what he wants from me. Once you become aware of what everybody else intuitively knows—the nonverbal signals you're sending that clearly mark your rule book— then you can evaluate whether that's how you want people to treat you and make changes accordingly.

All right, we've spent many pages giving you a lot of raw material. In the next chapter, let's begin to put everything together so that you can make some conclusions about who you are and how to maximize your strengths while working on your weaknesses.

# 8

## Is Life Working Out for You?

How satisfied are you, really, with where your life is going today?"

At first most people will answer that question with, "Well, it's okay, I guess." A few will come right out and say, "Doc, I gotta tell ya, my life is falling apart," but first-time meetings in my office usually don't start that way.

Yet I know the clients want something to change; otherwise, why would they be sitting in my office? And I think it's safe to say that I can make the same assumption about you. You must be hoping to change or address or at least better understand some aspect of your personality, or you wouldn't have spent the money to buy this book, nor would you have invested the amount of time required to read this far.

There's nothing wrong with that—the fact is, there are many things in my own life (a number of which I've already mentioned in this book) that I am working on. I admire people when they decide to make a change. But sometimes people need to be led to this realization. Here are a few typical examples.

"No, Dr. Leman," a female client says. "Everything is fine. I couldn't be happier. Sure, there have been some tough times, but overall, life has been wonderful."

"Okay," I respond. "So you're comfortable with the fact that you're thirty-one years old and have had three divorces, one bankruptcy, and a nervous breakdown?"

Or this:

"You've got it wrong, Dr. Leman. My life is pretty much together. I'm here to help my wife get straightened out, but there's nothing I need."

"Oh, really?" I respond. "Well then, can I ask you just one question?"

"Certainly."

"You're thirty years old, and you've already had four careers. Is that by design or is it a sign that the business world can't be perfect enough for you, that you haven't found your niche?"

People can live lives that outwardly show all the marks of chaos, disorganization, and even desperation, but for some reason they maintain an amazing sense of denial, as if nothing has ever been wrong.

What I hope to do with early childhood memories is show clients the themes that have led them into my office in the first place. If their first and second memories are both negative and their third memory reeks of "You didn't measure up! You're not good enough!" I can tell you these people aren't living a happy life. They feel oppressed, they're striving for something they'll never fully achieve, and they need to be released from the past that binds them. They may lie in the present, "Everything's fine!" but memories of their past reveal the truth.

I wish that, like a medical doctor, I could offer a simple prescription to make people feel better. "Dealing with low self-esteem? Here's a new drug called Oxy-esteem-alitis; take three tablets every day and you'll be just fine!" But counseling, of course, isn't like that. What I can do is help people see the dead ends they get themselves into, or at least help them to see that, yes, they are running around in circles all the time.

In essence, I'm trying to help clients develop the ability to stop and think things through and behave differently. It's analogous to rerouting a river—cutting a new tributary. At first this is very hard to do. Thousands of years of geologic formation are working against you, but once the new tributary is cut, the force of the river reinforces your new channel and everything flows smoothly.

The same thing takes place when we make over our personality. At first we encounter a lot of internal resistance. The force of twenty or thirty years' worth of personality ruts are working against us, but with patience we can eventually cut a new response, a new attitude, and a new behavior that, in time, will seem just as normal as the destructive response, attitude, or behavior used to seem.

Here's how to do that.

## Reprogramming Your Life

We're really starting to juggle several balls at once here, but let me do my best to help make everything clear. You were born with a certain disposition that was further cemented and solidified by your birth order and family environment. Consider these factors the "hardware" of your personality.

The "software" took over when things started happening in your life. You were just a little anklebiter, too small even to see over a coffee table, and with virtually no experience. You hadn't traveled to Europe; you weren't educated; you were plopped naked into this world, and from that point on, virtually every hour of every day, stimuli started hitting you across the head, and you had to make sense out of all of it: "What gets me noticed? Why do my parents treat me this way? How come my sister gets treated differently?"

You started making assumptions. You started answering the question that would shape your rule book: I only matter when _____. You weren't an adult when you made these conclusions. You didn't have a college degree. Your abstract thinking was nil. Still you came up with some definitive answers.

The problem is, they may not have been the right ones!

In short, to quote the apostle Paul, "When I was a child, I talked like a child, I thought like a child, I reasoned like a child" (1 Cor. 13:11). How could you do anything differently?

But notice that a change needs to occur. Paul goes on to say, "When I became a man, I put childish ways behind me."

You were bent as a child, but as an adult you have the opportunity to straighten out your bent nature. If you don't want to be a victim anymore, you don't have to be. It's actually healthy for you to admit, "You know what, I really have felt most comfortable when people pitied me, but I don't want to be pitied anymore. I want to be respected." That's maturity. That's thinking like a grown-up.

The pleaser may say, "Okay, I grew up thinking I only mattered when I was performing, but that's not true anymore. I want real intimacy based on true relationship. I want to be in a partnership where there is give-and-take." That's called growing up.

Let's look at how you can "unbend" your memories to rewrite your rule book.

## 1. Recognize That the Future Isn't a Prisoner of the Past

Many years ago, I worked with a Vietnamese girl. She was adopted into a very loving and caring American home, but she arrived on our shores with many painful scars— both physical and spiritual. I knew there was a lot of work to do when I inquired about the marks on her arms and she told me they were scars from cigarette burns—one of the worst forms of punishment I've ever come across in decades of counseling. We may never know all that went on in her early childhood.

Not surprisingly, my young client saw the world as a very hateful, hurtful, and spiteful place. Even after living in a warm and protected environment for far longer than she had lived in a horrendous one, she had a very difficult time breaking free from a terrible past.

I understood why this was so, but I wasn't about to let her stay there. Yes, she had some awful chapters in her life, but she needed to move on.

You do too. You're an adult now; you can discard what was done to you and begin to focus on how you'll be treated in the future.

For instance, as a toddler you may have been blamed more often than any of your siblings. You may have felt that you needed to control everything. You may have needed to please others to be accepted, but you don't have to stay stuck in any of these ruts. You can break out as an adult and say, "That's how I acted in the past. That's what

I believed when I was a child. But I'm not a child anymore, and I'm not going to keep acting that way."

You must separate the past from the future. The past has already influenced your present, but how much it influences your future is up to you.

### 2. Change Your Internal Dialogue

Self-talk is so important here. You can become your own best counselor—with the added benefit that talking to yourself won't cost you $125 an hour! My goal with all my clients is always the same: I want them to learn how to counsel themselves so that I'm no longer needed. My job is to give them the basic tools of psychology so they can treat themselves.

Don't misunderstand me: Damaged people need professionals. But even damaged people can eventually learn to take the tools they receive in counseling and strike out on their own. When you learn what we'll discuss in the final chapter—the importance of speaking positively about yourself, taking baby steps, marshaling your imaginative energy, giving yourself room to fail—you'll be ready to walk the road of emotional maturity. You can free your future from your past and begin to build on your strengths.

Avoid self-defeating talk. Comments like the following need to be chased out of your vocabulary:

"I have no restraint when it comes to food."

"I'm always making a mess of things."

"I'm the biggest loser in the world."

This type of internal dialogue only further cements the negative bent you received from your childhood. Here's a better form of internal dialogue:

"I've had problems with food in the past, but yesterday was a very good day, and today I've eaten responsibly in two out of three meals, with only one light snack. That's an improvement."

"In the past, I've failed at a couple of jobs. But now I've picked up some new interpersonal skills, and I really think I can make a go of it this time."

### 3. Become Your Own Parent

Now that you're an adult, you can talk to yourself like you are your own parent. The difference is that now you have experience. Now you have training. Now you understand how the world works, and out of all that maturity, you can do a better job shaping your own personality.

For instance, the controller can say, "It's scary for me to let others take charge, especially when I'm not sure they can do the job as well as I can. On the other hand, it's arrogant of me to assume that I'm the only one who knows how to do something. This attitude is causing stress in my marriage, negatively imprinting my kids, and giving me a reputation I don't enjoy. It's time to start changing."

Change will come in increments. When the controlling father lets his son wash the car, he is going to have to hold himself back from pointing out every little spot that Junior missed. No, Junior probably can't wash the car as well as Dad can, but so what? Are you entering your vehicle in some sort of spotless car contest?

What I'm urging you to do is to talk to yourself just like a good parent talks to his or her children. Build yourself up with positive and well-deserved encouragement. Be gentle with yourself when you fail. Learn to judge your behavior objectively and to correct it accordingly.

Don't just act, and don't just feel—think! Examine why you feel comfortable always being in control, always trying to please someone, always seeking someone to pity

143

you—and then remind yourself of why you don't want to play that role anymore.

## 4. Make a Bad Memory Good

When actor Jack Lemmon died in 2001, an article recounting his life caught my eye because one story within it was so similar to my own. Remember when I messed up a cheer as a little kid and made everybody laugh? Lemmon did the same thing, only it was in a play and not a cheer. He was eight years old, and because another kid got sick, Jack was asked to step in and help out with a school play. Jack got his first line right but messed up on the second one. His classmates started to laugh. What could have been a humiliating experience became a liberating one, however. Instead of fighting it, crying, or running away in embarrassment, Lemmon started milking the mistake for even more laughs. By the time he was done, the entire class applauded![1]

Looking back, Jack saw that incident as a turning point in his life. "I thought to myself, 'I think I like this.' This was the greatest day of my life."[2]

For many kids, getting laughed at by an entire class would be a humiliating day at best, but for Jack it was the start of something special. He had discovered his calling and used this gift to make the most of his career, ultimately appearing in more than five hundred TV shows and acting in some hilarious movies with one of his favorite sidekicks, Walter Matthau. They don't make comedies much better than *Grumpy Old Men*. Along the way, Lemmon won two Oscars and an Emmy.

There isn't a single person alive who doesn't harbor some very bad and even very painful memories. Consider one woman: As a child she experienced rape and poverty. Then she finally got a job at a local television station but was told by that same station that her nose, her hair, and her mouth were "all wrong." She went to a French hairdresser in New York City to try to do something about her hair and ended up going bald and getting scabs on her scalp!

Still she persisted, finally getting a chance to appear on Joan Rivers's show, where Rivers humiliated her by asking her why she was so fat. The fact that she could hear her own thighs rub together was enough to convince her to go to a fat farm to lose weight, but the visit was cut short when Steven Spielberg called to say he thought she would be perfect for the part of Sofia in a new movie he was filming called *The Color Purple*. The offer came with a warning, however. He said that if she lost one more pound, he might have to give the role to a different actress. Oprah Winfrey left the fat farm that day, stopping at a Dairy Queen on the way home.[3]

Successful people usually have as many bad memories as "regular" people do. In fact, they often have more. When a reporter asked Ernest Hemingway how to become a good writer, he responded, "Have a lousy childhood."

The difference is that successful people use their bad memories as motivation to create good memories. Jack Lemmon found something positive in making others laugh—even at his expense—and used it to become a famous actor. Oprah fought her way out of poverty and stereotyping to become America's favorite big sister.

Here's a secret you need to learn: The only power memories have to hold you back is the power you give them. Don't run from your memories; remember them! Cultivate them, reevaluate them, and then use them as motivation. Find out the positive side of each hurtful reminiscence. Even if something was truly terrible, such as Oprah's rape, your memory can be: "That was awful, but I survived." Even bad memories, looked at through this lens, can make us stronger.

For instance, let's take the situation my Vietnamese client faced. Instead of saying, "I was burned as a baby;

therefore the world is an awful place," she could say, "What was done to me was terrible. No baby should have to go through that. But I landed on my feet. God placed me in a loving family. Things changed, and there's no reason to believe they won't keep changing for the better."

A boy who missed an easy word at a spelling bee and was laughed at mercilessly can comfort himself by saying, "You know what? The pressure was on, I got nervous, and I missed an easy word. It can happen to anyone. In fact, it happened to a recent vice president. My worth isn't tied up in the fact that, as a second grader, I couldn't spell 'mitt.' It's time to move on."

The boy we mentioned earlier who was spanked in front of his friends could revisit his memories and say, "I bet Mom was really scared. And while it wasn't fair of her to blame me, and while it's true that I often got blamed for things I didn't do, I don't live with my mom anymore. When I go to work, they don't see me as the middle child; they see me as the accounts manager. I do good work, and my fear of failing is irrational. I haven't gotten a bad evaluation yet. In fact, my boss has been talking about a promotion and raise. I've really grown in my competence as a worker, and now it's time to grow emotionally as a person."

### 5. Forgive Your Parents

Our culture has made parent bashing a national sport. Rather than take responsibility for who we have become, we like to pawn off the blame on dysfunctional Dad and maniacal Mom.

Admittedly, as a counselor I've seen more than my share of parental horror stories. I'm not approaching this from a sentimental perspective. I know how cruel, vindictive, and downright hurtful some parents can be, but what I'm about to say is based on my experience working with children from very dysfunctional families: The worse your home life was, the more you need to forgive your parents.

Some of you have it backwards. You think that if your parents were average or maybe even slightly below average, you could forgive them. But if they're the bottom 10 percent, you could never forgive them. I believe it's just the opposite, because I believe forgiveness is one of the best tools you can use for emotional self-defense.

Dr. Lewis Smedes published a groundbreaking book in 1984 entitled *Forgive and Forget*. What made Dr. Smedes's book so different was his understanding that the first person served by forgiveness is the person who does the forgiving. Bitterness, prolonged anger, and resentment are emotional toxins. They poison our souls. Forgiveness is the great cauterizer; it burns away diseased emotions and frees us from the prison of the past.

I know what I'm talking about here. Neighbor kids used to call the gin mill my dad's office. I come from a long line of drinkers, and I've had my share of forgiving to do. I've learned that I will gain nothing and lose quite a bit if I hold on to the past and remain bitter and angry and spiteful.

When I encourage you to remember your early childhood memories, I want you to reject any false logic that has shaped you and also let go of what you need to forgive. Your parents may not deserve forgiveness, but you deserve the freedom that comes from the act of forgiving.

Perhaps you had good parents who occasionally messed up. Many parents don't need forgiveness as much as they need understanding. Nobody is perfect, and it's guaranteed that someone you live with for eighteen years or more will occasionally let you down or say something unkind. Don't resent your parents because they are human; understand their weakness and learn to love them as an adult.

I recommend to many of my clients that they initiate forgiveness by getting together with their parents (if the parents are still alive, of course). Sometimes, depending on the situation, personal contact is best avoided, but in most cases it can be very helpful to approach your parents as an adult and express that you want to build a new relationship with them, one that is based on mutual respect. You're not their little girl or little boy anymore, and if they're willing to treat you like the adult you are, you'd like to get to know them all over again.

### 6. Take Action

Psychological change doesn't mean squatting until you start putting it into action. *Change* is nothing more than an empty word unless you make the effort to implement the new insights you have received.

For example, a woman who has a habit of getting into destructive romantic relationships can say, "I'm not going to have sex anymore until I get married. I've got to make a change so that I can find someone who truly cares about me, not just someone who is looking out for his own pleasure."

The man who can't hold down a job can say, "The next time I get angry at my boss or the next time I'm told to do something that I think is stupid, I'm not going to quit. I've left too many good-paying jobs in the heat of the moment. From now on, the only way I'll leave a place of employment is through a written letter of resignation, giving me a chance to really think about my decision instead of just acting on emotion."

Real change won't take place until you think these thoughts and then put them into action.

### 7. Partner with Another Person

This sounds so simple, and yet it really is powerful: If you truly want to change, tell a friend about it and ask her to help you. "Arlene, I'm trying to shake Krispy Kremes; when we go out to have coffee, could you help remind me?"

When you're accountable to no one, you risk drifting with no port of call in sight. The drift might be slow, but a steady drift can take you a long way if it's not stopped. You can begin change right now by picking up the telephone and telling someone you want to change and enlisting their help. Public confession shows both you and others that you honestly mean business.

## The Next Step

We've spent a lot of time looking inward—at our temperaments, our family of origin, and our early memories. While it's important to do this from time to time, the irony is that real psychological health isn't achieved in isolation. People who are stuck on themselves and concerned only about themselves aren't healthy—they're obsessed. That's why the final section of this book will turn our eyes outward. How can we use what we know about ourselves to learn how to love others?

In other words, during this final section I want to teach you how to be a really great lover. Not Casanova—he was a jerk! I'm talking about a kind of love that will bring meaning, fulfillment, and joy into your life.

# PART 4

# LEARNING YOUR LOVE LANGUAGE

# 9

# What Fills Your Tank?

Just before our fifteenth wedding anniversary, I was walking around a store, thinking about what I should buy for Sande, when I came across the perfect present. There on the shelf in front of me sat the sleekest, most durable, and most beautiful toaster you have ever seen in your entire life. And it was a four-slicer! None of those puny two-slice toasters for my wife! It even had wide enough slots to toast bagels; what more could Sande ask for?

I bought the toaster and had the lady at the store wrap it up. "Is this a wedding present?" she asked.

"No," I said, "it's an anniversary present for my wife."

Much to my surprise, the nice lady kept shooting dirty glances my way. I assumed she was thinking about her own husband, wondering why he didn't have the good sense to get her such a fine gift. She must have been thinking, "Why couldn't I have had the good fortune to marry such a sensitive, creative man?"

Sande opened the present, said, "Oh, how nice," and put it in a prominent place in the kitchen. I felt all warm inside, knowing I had hit a home run.

Half an hour later, I noticed I hadn't seen Sande in a while. Well, to be honest, my then five-year-old son, Kevin, kind of gave me a clue.

"Dad," he asked, "why is Mommy crying in the bathroom with the door closed?"

I groaned, knowing I had made a mistake again. I thought I had learned. Early on in our marriage, I used to buy Sande underwear that she would never wear. She claimed, of all ridiculous things, that the kind I bought was "too uncomfortable." It took me a few years to discover that Sande's idea of comfortable panties bears a startling resemblance to maternity underwear. She thinks there needs to be room for two, even though she's a very slender woman.

Then there was the time I thought I should work more on romancing my wife, so I went to the department store and got Sande this knockout nightie. Man, was it hot.

Sande opened it, remarked at how pretty it was, kissed me on the cheek, and put it back in the box. That was the last time I saw that nightie until two years later, when I dug it up from the bottom of a ragbag with the faint aroma of lemon Pledge on it. To my knowledge, that nightie became the most expensive dust rag in the history of the world.

My gift-giving history (which has improved, by the way) is really just an exaggeration of how most of us act in relationships. We give others what we really want. It's almost a cliché—but a helpful one in this case—that the best present you can give to someone is to find something nearly identical to what they most recently gave to you.

You'll do yourself a major favor by understanding that different people like to be loved in different ways and through different means. What excites you and is mean-ingful to you may not be meaningful to others. Having this understanding will help you further define your own unique qualities as well as help you to explain yourself to others. It will also help you learn how to love people who are special to you in a way that produces more inti-mate relationships.

Learning to love doesn't come naturally to any of us; it's a skill we need to learn. Fortunately, there's help. My friend Gary Chapman has done us all a great favor by writing a wonderful book with great take-away value that every-body should read, even those who aren't married: *The Five Love Languages: How to Express Heartfelt Commitment to Your Mate*. After more than two decades as a marriage counselor, Gary has identified five emotional love lan-guages. Though each language may have several additional "dialects," every person's emotional needs can be under-stood through these five basic labels.

As a psychologist, I have particular appreciation for what Gary has written, in large part because his five languages really have covered every individual I've met and with whom I've worked. This is a very helpful and practical sys-tem that I believe everyone ought to learn.

Here's the trick: It is rare for a husband and wife to share the same love language. Consequently, the young inexpe-rienced wife will often love her husband just how *she* wants to be loved—and leave her husband's emotional tank empty as a result. The frustrated husband will in turn love his wife just how *he* wants to be loved, hoping she'll get the hint. Of course, she doesn't, because she can't imagine why her husband is treating her the way he is. She doesn't want to be loved like that, so there's no way she's going to love her husband that way.

If you've been excited learning about yourself and find yourself groaning and asking, "Why do I need to study emo-tional love languages?" let me be very frank. Behind every failed marriage, rebellious kid, or broken relationship is an empty love tank. I remember one client who came to see me, exhausted by the emotional distance in her marriage. Both she and her husband worked all the time, and I remember thinking, *This woman is a prime candidate for an affair.*

I felt it was my duty to point out to her that all the warning signs were present for marital infidelity, but I decided to take an indirect approach. I asked her, "Have you been tempted to have an affair?"

She almost laughed. "Already been there and done that," she confessed. "How'd you know?"

Stupid me, I thought it *might* happen, and it already had!

I'm not saying an empty love tank is the only explanation for marital breakdown and juvenile delinquency, but it's often a contributing factor. If you want to have a successful, happy life and a healthy home, it's vital that you learn to speak your loved one's love language.

There's an added benefit of course: As you study these languages, you'll find out how *you* want to be loved. No longer will you have to hope your husband or wife figures it out on their own. You'll be able to describe for them exactly what makes you feel loved.

For the singles who are reading this book, I encourage you to take this love language business rather seriously. If you know how you like to be loved, you'll be better prepared to choose a suitable mate. For instance, if your love language is having someone spend quality time with you, don't marry a Type A, Wall Street kind of guy. You'll just frustrate him and hurt yourself. If your love language is hearing words of affirmation, don't marry the silent brooding type.

I realize this type of thinking might sound cold and unromantic to some of you, but I think it makes great sense. If you want a cuddly dog that will sit quietly on your lap, don't keep looking at Dobermans. If you want a dog that will protect you, stay away from the toy poodles. I don't subscribe to the theory that there's just one person made for each one of us and that "destiny" will bring us together. I think most of us could be happily married to hundreds of people if we'd just focus on compatibility and common sense. (For more on this, see my book *The Birth Order Connection*.)

Let's look at Dr. Chapman's five love languages.

## Love Language #1: Words of Affirmation

Silence is never golden for people whose love language is words of affirmation. There are certain members of the human race who live for an aptly spoken compliment, a tender word of endearment, or an uplifting encouragement. You can do all sorts of positive things for these individuals—make them a nice meal, give them a hearty hug, spend long hours in their presence—but if you don't verbalize your affection and commitment, they won't feel loved.

I call words of affirmation "slipping your kids commercial messages." In my practice, I've heard more than my share of negative, critical parenting, and I've witnessed firsthand the devastating destruction that harsh, critical parenting can do. Perhaps because of this experience, I go out of my way to provide encouraging commentaries that build up my kids: "Honey, taking you and your friends home from the ice skating rink reminded me of what a good job you've done choosing your friends; they're wonderful girls, every one of them, and I'm proud of the decisions you've made."

Or to the son who has been struggling with his swing and finally gets a hit: "Well, Tommy, it looks like that practice is really paying off!"

My friend Moonhead and I were in a restaurant recently when we saw a guy wearing a shirt that made me chuckle. Since I used to play golf, I could relate. The shirt had four lines:

"I hate golf."

"I hate golf."

"Nice shot, buddy."

"I love golf."

One positive phrase can completely transform a frustrating ordeal!

Keep in mind, however, that I'm not talking about empty praise, which I think can be destructive. I'm speaking of meaningful encouragement, noticing a trait in the child or spouse or friend and saying, "That's a trait to hold on to and build upon."

This love language often produces the most trouble in a marriage when it's a love language favored by the wife, in large part because men aren't that good with words. We're great with noises, grunts, and commands, but terms of endearment? Well, we could do better. On average, men use three times fewer words per day than women. By the time most of us men get home from work, 99 percent of our words are used up. I've never met a man who told me that, coming home from a long day at the office, his first thought was, *What I could really use is a good forty-five-minute talk with my wife.* Such a man may exist, but I haven't met him yet! Given this, it's not difficult to see how women who feel loved primarily through words of affirmation might feel shortchanged in many marriages.

If you're a man reading this, may I suggest that you need to reconsider your silence out of love for your wife and kids? I've counseled a surprising number of men who told me, "Look, Dr. Leman, I made a promise to my wife on our wedding day, and I intend to keep it."

"What was your promise?"

"I told her that I loved her very much and that if things ever changed, she'd be the first to know. In the meantime, unless I bring it up again, she doesn't need to worry about whether I love her. She can remember what I told her on our wedding day."

Sorry, buddy, but that's not gonna cut it if your wife's love language is words of affirmation. She needs to hear it again and again and again.

Your marriage isn't like an old-growth forest; it's a newly planted garden. Old-growth forests are pretty sturdy. They don't need to be watered. They don't need to be weeded. If we don't pollute them, poison them, or burn them down, they're going to do just fine.

A garden, on the other hand, is the exact opposite. If you don't water it, if you don't make sure it gets enough sunlight, if you don't weed it and care for it and fertilize it, you won't get squat. You'll have a salad with one puny carrot and a bug-infested head of lettuce.

Your marriage is like that garden. One watering won't last for fifty years. You need to water your marriage every day, sometimes every hour.

So, men, if words of affirmation constitute your wife's love language, let me help you apply this advice. Your wife needs for you to take some words and do something that might not seem natural to you, but think of it as a building project, only this time you're going to build a sentence. A sentence requires many things, including a subject, a verb, and an object. "Huh?" "What?" "I dunno," and "Whatever" do *not* qualify as sentences for this discussion. The sentences I'm talking about go like this:

"I love you more today than I ever have; life with you just keeps getting sweeter."

"You're so good to me; how could I ever make it without you?"

"I was feeling a little down today, so I just started thinking about you. That made me feel a whole lot better."

Any one of the above statements can be uttered in ten seconds or less, but each one can literally be a highlight of your wife's week if the words are said with sincerity.

For those men who have a hard time expressing themselves, I suggest you use a word picture. Men often aren't very good with feelings, but we can do better with images: "I'm so angry I feel like a dog trying to tear apart a raw steak." "I feel like the weight of the world has been put on my shoulders, and I'm too tired to keep standing up." "At work I feel like I have two strikes against me and an umpire who hates me; there's no way I can avoid striking out."

I know some of you may feel uncomfortable talking about fears, emotions, or dreams, but that's okay. This isn't about you—it's about your spouse, making her feel loved, cherished, and fulfilled. If you have to be occasionally uncomfortable to achieve that, so be it.

Gary Chapman recommends uttering words of affirmation in front of your spouse when others are present and also in front of others when your spouse is not present. The kind words are likely to get back to your spouse and will make her feel loved all the more when she hears how you have been talking about her, in a positive sense, behind her back.

One thing is particularly important if your spouse's love language is words of affirmation: Drop all negatives. Complaining and nagging won't do a thing for you. The funny thing I've learned about people who have a verbal love language is this: While positive words rev them up like nothing else, negative comments bring them as low as they can get. Just as they are unusually sensitive to praise, they are extremely sensitive to criticism. They usually just shut down.

If your love language is verbal and you're single, find a man or woman who knows how to communicate verbally. If you're married to a person whose love language is verbal, you simply have to develop the skills of conversation; that's the only way your spouse will feel loved.

## Love Language #2: Quality Time

I had a mom come to me once, frustrated with her relationship with her oldest daughter. She went out of her way to verbally engage her daughter but seemed to get nowhere. Her husband, on the other hand, was the silent brooding type who rarely spoke, but he had the daughter's undying devotion and affection.

Mom just couldn't understand how this quiet man could have captured his daughter's heart when she, who peppered her daughter with questions, seemed to get nowhere.

I spent some time talking to the daughter and immediately picked up on the problem.

When the parents and I got back together, I asked the mom a couple simple questions:

"When your daughter has a hard time getting to sleep, what CD does she like to listen to?"

"I don't know."

"New Kids on the Block," Dad answered.

"Right," I said.

"How did you know that, dear?" Mom asked her husband.

"Because sometimes she asks me to put it on when I leave the room."

I continued, "When your daughter is at the plate while playing softball, what does she do?"

Mom looked dumbfounded.

"She hits the plate twice with the bat when she's feeling confident, but she looks back at me when she's feeling nervous," Dad said.

This daughter's love language was quality time. Dad gave her that time; Mom gave her only words. The questions Mom peppered her with didn't feel like affirmation to begin with; they felt like the grand inquisition. By and large, adolescents don't like questions. Given this, it was

161

only natural that the daughter felt closer to her dad; he loved her the way she wanted to be loved.

One of the best ways for me to show love to one of my daughters is to sit down and listen to her new CDs. I happen to be a Dixie Chicks fan, so it doesn't take much sacrifice when the girls buy their latest CD, but love for my daughters is the *only* reason I've ever sat down to hear *NSYNC and the Backstreet Boys croon their way to another best-selling CD. Even when my daughters come up with something I don't like at all, as long as it's not offensive, I find one positive thing about it and mention that: "Well, it's got a good beat," or, "That woman has a knockout voice."

Some spouses and kids couldn't care less about receiving gifts—they want your time. They want you to sit with them, take walks with them, go to ball games with them, watch a movie with them, or just get home in time to eat dinner with them. It doesn't cost you money to do this: They aren't necessarily asking to spend time at the beach, a resort, or a palace—they just want you by their side.

Kids who have this love language want you at their games. It's not the same if you get too busy, miss the game, and then offer to sit down and listen to a recap. They want to look up in the stands and see you there. If they're singing in the choir, they don't care if you can't make out their voices. Their love tank feels full when they catch sight of your familiar face as they look out into the audience.

Sande really touched my heart just a few years into our marriage when she showed up to watch me receive my doctorate degree. That may not sound like much to you, but consider the circumstances: I received my degree on a Saturday afternoon, and on Thursday night (about thirty-six hours previously), Sande had given birth to our second daughter, Krissy. Sande was still in a wheelchair, but she made it to the ceremony, and it meant so much to me that she offered such a heroic effort to watch me get my doctorate.

Sometimes religious people are the world's worst at giving their time to their loved ones. So many well-meaning men and women get involved in leadership to the point of exhaustion; they're out four or even five nights a week, all in the name of doing God's work. The real result of this overinvolvement is that they frequently abandon their own families. Unfortunately, pastors, deacons, and layleaders often try to defend this abandonment by wrapping it in spirituality and "serving God." When you talk to the families that get left behind, however, you see firsthand how destructive overinvolvement can be.

If your spouse or kids have quality time as their primary love language, you must learn to become ruthless with your schedule. If you don't draw up some guidelines, overinvolvement will wreck your family. I have a great little exercise to help overinvolved families. Right off the bat, I'll tell them to list everything everyone is involved in. The list can become almost humorous if the consequences weren't so dire. I've seen some boys play on three different baseball teams—during the same season. I've had dads off golfing while mom is riding horses and the kids are farmed out all over the city.

Once the list is laid in front of me, I give them a marker and say, "All right, cut out half of it."

"You've got to be kidding!" they'll protest.

"I'm not. You must cut down your activities by 50 percent."

Some of these families are like alcoholics—they're so busy they truly don't understand the stress behind what they're doing. They can get desperate when they're finally urged to make some choices and to realize that sometimes you have to pass up even some very profitable activities to avoid becoming too busy.

Once the painful cuts are made, my next advice is to get them to write a little saying on a note card and put that card by the phone. The saying goes like this: "If there's any doubt, say no." Too-busy people have faulty filters. In the back of their minds, they get little warnings, "Does Susan really have time to do one more activity?" but then the mom starts rationalizing and thinking about what her daughter will "miss out on," and before you know it, the already tired kid has just been signed up for her tenth weekly commitment. In my book, if there's any doubt at all, respond by cutting it out. Unless you can absolutely defend spending time on this activity, get rid of it.

I don't mean this to sound like a warning, but in many ways it really is: If you don't spend quality time with a person who has this love language, they won't feel loved, and we live in a day and age in which many waiting arms are available for neglected people. In case I'm not being specific enough, I'll be even more direct: Your spouse will eventually find someone who wants to spend time with her; if it's not you, she'll hook up with someone else. Your teenage son will find a young girl and maybe get her pregnant, or he'll start hanging out with a drug-taking gang of guys if his family is too busy to create a sense of belonging. The person who truly stands alone is one in a trillion. Almost all of us keep looking until we find someone who wants to be in our presence.

For the person who feels loved by time, quantity can't be ignored. The old saw about quality time won't make up for a lack of quantity; kids just don't think that way.

However, it is important in the midst of providing a generous quantity of time to also carve out *meaningful* time. In other words, watching TV together may boost CBS's ratings, but it won't mean squat to your kid or spouse. Reading a newspaper at the breakfast table puts you in the same room but on an entirely different planet. Having the radio on while you drive in the car together doesn't create any communal memories.

Meaningful time doesn't happen by accident; you have to choose it. You're going to have to motivate yourself to turn off the television, go outside, and shoot baskets with your son. Instead of running off by yourself, maybe you can shock the family by suggesting you all get together and play Yahtzee or Monopoly. Or perhaps you can tell the kids to finish up the dishes and then take your wife by the hand, telling her, "Come on, honey, let's go for a walk. I want to hear about your day."

While you're spending time, Dr. Chapman recommends the following:[1]

1. Maintain eye contact when your spouse is talking.
2. Don't do something else while talking to your spouse.
3. Listen for feelings.
4. Observe body language.
5. Refuse to interrupt.

You'll also want to focus on occasional quality events. If your husband is a big baseball fan, maybe you could buy two tickets and surprise him, even if nine innings sounds eight innings too long. If your daughter loves jazz dance, take her to a performance, even if you think dancing is boring. If your wife is a big fan of art and you hear about the local museum getting a new exhibition, bring it up first. It will mean so much more to your loved one that you brought it up and you were the initiator, rather than reluctantly responding to his or her request.

## Love Language #3: Receiving Gifts

All right, you already know gift giving isn't my strong suit, but in my defense, my wife isn't exactly the easiest person to buy gifts for. She has her own store in Tucson called the "Shabby Hattie," where she sells things affectionately known as "shabby chic." In other words, it's stuff that people used to throw away but now pay top dollar to acquire. What she likes most she puts in her own store, but I can't buy presents *for* my wife *from* my wife! She won't give me credit!

While we were summering in upstate New York, my wife came across some old beat-up fence boards. Naturally Sande thought someone would love to pay a good bit of money to buy these old boards and use them to decorate, so she stored them outside until she could take them back to Tucson. The boards couldn't get any more beat-up than they already were, so there was no need to cover them.

About the same time, we had a rather colorful man come to clean out our septic tank. I'm not sure of all that made up this guy's history, but any man with just seven fingers certainly has a few stories to tell.

He drove into our yard, started cleaning out the septic tank, and then found that his truck was full and needed to be emptied before he could finish the job. He didn't want to leave the septic tank open, so he looked around our yard to see if there were any worthless objects that he could use to cover the hole.

Guess what he found . . .

Tastes differ, but what we give and how we receive gifts says an awful lot about us. The best gift Sande ever gave me, besides my jukebox, was one that she had made. She had taken the cover from my very first book, framed it, and put a gold plate on the bottom that read, "Number one husband, number one father, number one author." The whole thing couldn't have cost her more than twenty dollars, but to me, it's priceless.

Gary Chapman writes, "A gift is something you can hold in your hand and say, 'Look, he was thinking of me,' or, 'She remembered me.' You must be thinking of someone to give him a gift. The gift itself is a symbol of that thought. It doesn't matter whether it costs money. What is important is that you thought of him. And it is not the thought implanted only in the mind that counts, but the thought expressed in actually securing the gift and giving it as the expression of love."[2]

If you are married to someone whose love language is receiving gifts, you need to get creative, within your budget, at finding gifts. A good gift might be a flower, a prized baseball card, tickets to a game or the opera; the gift could be free or costly, but it needs to be a gift. Wives, you might think that doing everything at home and then some is enough, but if your husband is a gift receiver, he'll feel slighted. Men, you might think that providing an income such that your wife can choose to work or not, getting a spacious home, and having late-model vehicles speaks for itself in regard to your affection, but if your wife's love language is receiving gifts, she'll feel nothing but emotional distance in that new house and new car. Fill both of them up with visual symbols of your love!

If you're single and you like to receive gifts, don't marry a self-obsessed man or a man with little creativity. Here's a clue, by the way: However creative he is while dating, divide that creativity in half and that's what you can expect in marriage. If you're already disappointed with this guy while still single, don't even think about marrying him. He won't improve, regardless of what he says.

To show a woman this kind of love, you need to get to know her. For starters, you need to understand her well enough to know if she would think something is tacky or endearing. Is she motivated by the price and the place of purchase or by the thought behind it? Does she care if you remember that yellow roses are her favorite, or is she happy to get any flowers because the mere act of giving something shows you were thinking about her?

When Kevin was just four years old, he absolutely melted Sande's heart, even though his act was blatant thievery. He woke up one morning, took a tour of the neighborhood, and helped himself to our fellow residents' most colorful flowers. He then walked into the kitchen and handed his mommy a precious bouquet. Sande was purring for hours (though I noticed she put the flowers in a place where they couldn't be seen from outside).

Just as thoughtful gifts can work wonders, so wrong-headed gifts can hurt people deeply. When a dad buys his daughter an age-inappropriate gift—getting a sixteen-year-old a Kate and Ashley videotape, for instance, just because she liked the twins as a preadolescent—his daughter feels misunderstood, insulted, and unloved. To truly give a gift well, the gift must be given out of understanding and intimacy.

I'd like to make one other point before we move on. Sometimes love requires us to receive a gift rather than just give a gift. I've come across martyr types who are very selfish people. Though they are always doing things for others, they don't allow anyone to do anything for them. While this seems generous, they are actually denying others the pleasure they receive from giving.

If your spouse, friend, or family member likes to give gifts, learn how to receive them—for their sake, not yours. You might indeed use the nightie as a dust rag or the ghastly tie as something with which to wipe off your car's oil dipstick, but be gracious. Receiving gifts can be just as important as giving gifts.

## Love Language #4: Acts of Service

I have a friend who travels a good bit and whose wife hates the thought of gas stations. It's like she's allergic to them. She'll drive a car on fumes for six months before she'll go through a self-serve line. Before most of his trips, one of his last acts is to check the gas gauge on the family minivan. If it's below half a tank, he makes sure he fills it up.

What he may not realize is that he's filling more than a gas tank—he's also filling his wife's love tank. Some people respond best to concrete acts of service. Even things like changing the cat's litter box or scooping up dog droppings in the backyard can seem almost romantic to the person for whom it is done.

If you're a woman and your love language is acts of service, you probably feel most loved when your husband or boyfriend fixes your plumbing, changes the oil in your car, or helps you put together something you bought from Costco. If you're a man, you may feel most loved when your wife or girlfriend bakes you special treats or saves you the hassle of shopping for clothes by picking up something for you to wear.

I have another friend who is more of the literary sort. He majored in English at college, likes words, and even used to write poetry. He has tried to love his wife with words of affirmation, using creative phrases rather than stock clichés, and one time his wife responded, "Oh, good one, Jim!" She admired his creativity, but it didn't really touch her heart.

He also tried buying her creative gifts, such as a Japanese buckwheat pillow and special health food treats. She appreciates them, but they don't overwhelm her, even when he guesses correctly that she would truly enjoy something.

What she really likes most is what her husband hates: replacing the leaking toilet, fixing a broken hinge, hanging up a heavy mirror.

When they moved into a new house, she bought a living room mirror that weighed about sixty pounds. Jim was afraid to hang it because he knew if he hung it, it would eventually fall down and break. That mirror sat against the wall of the living room for three months, and every day it stayed there the wife felt a little more frustrated and a little less loved. She didn't want words. She didn't want any gifts. She wanted the stupid mirror hung.

And when Jim finally broke down and got a friend to help him do it right, she rewarded him that night in a very intimate and creative way. He had been married for five years until he finally began to realize what really makes his wife feel loved—and what makes her want to love him back!

People who love acts of service tend to be less sentimental and far more practical than the words or gifts crowd. All that romance is fine for an occasional diversion, but the bread and butter on which they want to exist consists of doing practical things that make their lives easier.

I know I'm going to sound repetitious here, but again, I want singles to consider this as part of the dating experience. Women, if you know this is your love language and you marry a guy who got a doctorate degree in early American literature but who couldn't put together a twelve-piece puzzle, much less a desk from Costco, think twice. If you're a single man with this love language, don't marry a lazy, ditzy woman. Marry someone who has the initiative and ability that is so important to you.

## Love Language #5: Physical Touch

I had a client who was probably better fed than any husband I've ever met. His wife loves to cook, and when I say cook, I don't mean heat up some store-bought lasagna. She is of the crowd that thinks presentation is as important as taste, so she plans dinners not just by their taste and nutritional content but by how the various colors will look on the plate.

She's Martha Stewart's twin. Her husband's closet is so organized it gives me a headache just looking at it. Every shoe has its place, and virtually every sock and piece of underwear has been inventoried and catalogued.

He never forgets one of his relative's birthdays or anniversaries, because his Martha Stewart wife reminds him precisely three weeks before each event. If he hasn't done anything with that information, she gives him a reminder at two weeks. If he tarries another day or two, she presents him with three card options and asks him to sign one.

I don't know that any man has ever been taken care of quite so well; even so, he ended up in my office, frustrated at the tremendous lack of love he felt in his marriage. His wife couldn't understand his sense of alienation. What more could she do for him?

I'll tell you what I told her: She could touch him. Anywhere, at any time, and at virtually any place. He wanted physical affection. Without that touch, he would never feel loved.

Gary Chapman writes, "Physical touch can make or break a relationship. It can communicate love or hate. To the person whose primary love language is physical touch, the message will be far more than the words 'I hate you' or 'I love you.' A slap in the face is detrimental to any child, but it is devastating to a child whose primary love language is touch. A tender hug communicates love to any child. But it shouts love to the child whose primary love language is physical touch. The same is true of adults."[3]

There's an incredible power in the simple touch for both sexes; many women absolutely love to be touched (not grabbed but touched). Men aren't that much different. For 90 percent of us, if you want to get our attention, just touch us. You can touch us anywhere—any part of the body is good! (Okay, some places are more special than others.) When women ask me how they can get their husbands to listen to them, I usually encourage them to use touch before and while they talk. That gets hubby's (or boyfriend's) attention. Kiss the back of his neck, put your arm inside his, gently nibble at his ear. He's all yours. Then,

171

as you're touching him, you can slip him the commercial announcement you want him to hear.

Try it and see; for most men, this approach works far better than buying your husband a Miracle Ear. Plus, it's a lot cheaper and you won't have to keep batteries lying around the house.

Touching works just as well with friends of the same sex. At my dad's funeral, Bill Foster, one of my best friends, never said a word to me. He just walked up to me and touched me. That's all he had to do; I knew exactly how he felt and exactly what he was saying.

This is an area where many women completely miss their husbands. They do so many things for their husband and their family, but they don't realize that inside this big man is a person dying to be needed. I'm not talking about wanting to be needed by people at work but by his wife. What makes him feel needed? A clean house? No. A good meal? No. Those things make him feel served, but not needed. What makes most men feel needed and wanted is when their wives show an assertive and aggressive sexual interest.

I know, I know—some women are dismissing this advice as fast as they read it, but trust me—I think the divorce statistics speak for themselves. Most men today do not feel needed. They are looking for significance, and fewer and fewer are finding that significance in the workplace. If a woman will really work at being tuned in to the fact that men need to feel needed and that physical touch is a big part of that, they will increase the probability of becoming one with their mate.

Men, you need to know that your wife wants a giving touch—that is, women want an occasional touch that isn't tied to a sweaty and naked agenda. So often I hear women complain that what they really wanted to do was just hug their husband and give him a quick peck, but hubby got the wrong idea; the next thing the wife knows, her clothes are off and she's looking at the ceiling thinking, *This isn't exactly what I had in mind.*

Touch your wife gently, adoringly, and without asking for any touch in return. Take her hand on the occasional walk; slow down long enough to give her a quick peck on the cheek. When she hugs you, hug her back. When she's sad or lonely or just tired, hold her, rub her feet, or just sit quietly next to her with your arm around her.

Parents, I need to share a few words with you too. Dr. Harry Schaumburg, who works with leaders on the problems of sexual misconduct and sexual addiction, warns, "Nearly all the sex addicts I've counseled have shared with me that their parents—or the people who raised them—were 'cold,' 'distant,' or 'didn't show much affection.' Through the years I've realized that appropriate physical touch plays a vital role in developing intimacy in relationships and in teaching appropriate physical boundaries, too. People tend to thrive physically and emotionally when they are nurtured with appropriate human touch. It helps to provide affirmation of love and acceptance as well as physical comfort."[4]

Touch has the power to do great harm or to communicate healthy affection. No less a teacher than Jesus used touch in powerful ways.

It was tough enough being a woman in the first century, but being a bleeding woman was the doorway to destitution. For starters, such a woman could forget about intimacy. Jewish laws prescribed that anyone who came into contact with such a woman would be unclean. But there was a desperate woman in the first century who had been bleeding for twelve years. As Jesus walked by, she reached out to him.

According to the New Testament, Jesus stopped walking, which grabbed the crowd's attention. He then called out, "Who touched me?" Having sensed that "power had gone out from him," he waited until the bleeding woman came forward. The last thing your average first-century rabbi would do if touched by a bleeding woman would be to call attention to it. But even if the rare rabbi were to do this, surely he wouldn't use the bleeding woman as a role model! But Christ did. He extolled her faith publicly: "Daughter, your faith has healed you" (Luke 8:40–48; Mark 5:25–34).

Christ touched the untouchable. He didn't just include them in his teaching. He didn't just send them money. He touched them. And in doing this, he provided a tremendous example of how to make others feel truly and deeply loved.

## How Do I Know?

Some of you are thinking, *How can I figure out my spouse's or kid's love language when they won't talk to me, or when they don't even know it themselves?* I've got a pretty simple exercise to get this information: Ask yourself, *What does this person complain about most?*

Nine times out of ten, that complaint will revolve around the person's love language. I've picked this up in the counseling room. "Jerry's very good to me, Dr. Leman—he brings me presents all the time, he fixes whatever gets broken, but he just never wants to sit with me. I can't tell you how much that hurts!"

I know right away that that woman's love language is quality time, not receiving gifts or acts of service.

Later in the afternoon, a woman will tell me, "Bob is happy to follow me around, but I wish he'd fix the broken lamp instead!" Right away, I know she wants to be loved with acts of service, not quality time.

If we open our ears to our loved ones, they'll let us know how they want to be loved. Better yet, why not have a meaningful conversation at dinner tonight? If it's just you and your husband, or you and your boyfriend, or maybe your entire family (with kids), why not bring this book to the table, describe each love language, and ask each person to pick the one that means the most to them?

Keep in mind that your goal is to learn how to love someone by expressing intimacy in a way that he or she can receive it. Any of the love languages can be used to manipulate rather than love, but some are more open to abuse than others. I've seen some individuals supposedly love with acts of service; the problem is, these acts become a panacea for those who have a difficult time being intimate with words or through touch. Giving gifts can have a built-in distance: "I'll give you flowers, but I won't talk to you; I won't give you myself." I'm not degrading these love languages. I just want you to be careful about how they can be misused.

For your own self-care, increased understanding of the love languages will help you understand what you want and need. You might be a combination; you might be solidly in one camp. But it truly does help to know how you like to be loved.

# 10

## This Book Should Cost $125

Wayne Carlson got off to a bad start; unfortunately, he never wised up and consequently turned a bad start into a bad habit that cost him three decades of living.

Carlson's bad start erupted from a 1960 arrest and conviction for car theft. He was just barely an adult—eighteen years old—when he was sentenced to one year at Saskatchewan's Prince Albert Penitentiary for his crime.

One year can seem like a long time to an eighteen-year-old. Jail is a rough place to live. For instance, cigarettes are forbidden, so the only way you can light one (they smuggle them in) is to wrap a fork with toilet paper and jam it into an exposed socket (hopefully without killing yourself in the process).

After several months, Carlson had had enough and decided to escape. He was successful but was later recaptured and sentenced to a longer period of time for escaping. The longer sentence only made Carlson more determined to get out of jail, so he escaped again. This went on for a North American record of thirteen prison escapes. Carlson's initial one-year sentence eventually stretched into a three-decade ordeal.[1]

The famous definition of insanity is doing the same thing again and again while expecting different results. When it comes to personality change, many of us are like Wayne Carlson. We keep making the same mistakes, making a bad situation worse and often ruining our lives in the process.

Do you know why people are willing to part with $125 an hour to talk with a psychologist? They've made bad decisions. It's as simple as that. And the reason many are willing to keep paying $125 an hour for months on end is that they keep making bad decisions and need an objective voice to help them break the pattern.

Reading this book isn't going to do you one bit of good if you keep making the same kind of poor decisions you've made in the past. If you change your choices, however, this book is easily worth $125—the cost of one session with a top psychologist. One of the reasons I wanted to write this book, to be honest with you, is to use it with clients. It'll save both their time and mine if clients can first grasp these basic issues before we spend our far more expensive time together fine-tuning their application.

I don't want to sound harsh, but I'm sick and tired of hearing women in their late twenties come crying to me about how "life has been so unfair" because the guy they moved in with dumped them for another chick—after he created a baby. The fact is, they made a bad decision, and now they're going to have to live with the consequences. If they keep hooking up with these guys, before long they'll have three or four kids, all of whom will have different fathers (none of whom can afford to make child payments, of course). By their fourth or fifth decade, their looks will have waned, they'll be left alone, and they'll think this world is terribly cruel and unfair.

I'm sorry, but it's not so much that this world is unfair as that they made some awful choices.

I don't know if I can listen to too many more men who broke up their families for a younger woman or just midlife freedom and now seem surprised and even angry that their kids are displaying all the signs of insecurity and abandonment. They want me to fix their kids when I want to fix them!

So how do you turn the knowledge we've talked about into choices? I believe the most powerful method of change is learning to depend on God and receive his power. As a psychologist, I believe it is also extremely helpful and important to have accurate self-knowledge. People who keep making the same mistakes usually have an ideal view of themselves that never squares with reality. They base their choices on faulty assumptions and thus make poor choices.

Hopefully all that we have discussed has given you greater insight not only into who you are but why you are that way. What do you do with that information now? This is where we get into the fun part: applying what we've learned.

## Relationships

Whether you're married or single, understanding birth order, temperament, love languages, and early childhood memories can play a valuable role in teaching you both how to love and how to find the right person to love. This information can help you be a better parent as well.

179

## Singles

Let's talk to the singles first. I want you to look back on your life and ask yourself, *When it comes to relationships, how have I done?* If your relational life is a mess, I'm willing to bet that you have based most of your previous decisions on feelings. You were convinced that this man or this woman was "the one," your destined soul mate. The tingling way you felt when you first kissed convinced you that "this is the person I'm going to spend the rest of my life with."

Are you willing to try something different? To some of you, this will sound very unromantic, but if you'll just listen to me, I can help you make a much better choice when you consider another—or your first—life partner.

For instance, let's say you're a last born. I want you to think carefully about what will make a good marriage partner. You know your weaknesses: You likely have a difficult time reining in your compulsive tendencies. You probably like to be on center stage or at least cared for. You may have a special gift for spending money—even, on occasion, money you don't have.

Tell me: What will happen if you marry someone just like you—that is, another last born? Nine times out of ten, disaster! You'll be broke; the house will erupt into chaos; the bills will go unpaid; and your happy-go-lucky nature will take a severe downslide into discouragement, perhaps even depression.

As a last born myself, I can tell you that one of the best decisions I've ever made was to marry my first-born wife. My rule of thumb concerning birth order is this: Marry your opposite. Two first borns create more sparks than the Fourth of July. Two last borns may have a lot of initial fun but eventually lose their way. Two middle borns may never be able to make a decision without worrying about offending the other person.

180

This means that the ideal marriage arrangements are last born–first born or last born–only. What about the middles? Middle children are like Type O blood—they go along with just about anything, except perhaps another middle. Keep in mind, there are different types of middles. A middle-born man who also happens to be the oldest son might be a very good choice for a last-born wife— but the same guy may butt heads with a first-born wife. A middle-born woman who is the youngest girl in her family could be an ideal match for a first-born male—but maybe not the best choice for a last-born male.

Look at the entire family situation and learn to make a wise choice. Marry your opposite and you can't go too far wrong.

The same principle holds true for sanguines, phlegmatics, cholerics, and melancholies. In general, you'll do better by marrying your opposite. Some phlegmatics get along better with sanguines—their quiet peaceful nature relies on somebody else who has spunk—while other phlegmatics may prefer cholerics or melancholies who will take charge.

You'll see sparks fly or gaps arise if two cholerics get hooked up—or two sanguines, two melancholies, and so on. I've already stated that I see most last borns as sanguines, most middle borns as phlegmatics, most melancholies as only children, and most cholerics as first borns. This isn't 100 percent accurate, of course, so learn to look at yourself in balance—a last born with sanguine tendencies but also bent toward being a choleric, for instance. If that's the case, consider marrying a phlegmatic. If you're a last born with phlegmatic tendencies, look for a melancholy or choleric.

Before the romantics start howling at how unromantic this sounds, let me just say this: I have counseled—formally and informally—thousands of couples, almost all of whom were deeply in love, head over heels about each other, giddy at the thought of spending the rest of their lives together. The romance was there; the sexual chemistry was high; they couldn't keep their hands off each other.

But they made a bad match. Once the infatuation wore off—and it always will—they were left with an ill-considered choice and a difficult marriage.

I'm not suggesting that some form of attraction isn't necessary. As a single, I enjoyed a good bout of infatuation as much as anybody. But before I commit my life to another person, I want to make sure the compatibility will last past the intense emotions. Because of that, I'm going to compare our families of origin. I'll look at birth order. I'll consider temperaments. I'll ask myself, *Is this a good match on paper?*

Then I'll delve into their early childhood memories. I want to know if they are a controlling person, a pleaser, a charmer, or a victim. I want to see whether they view this world as a safe place, a happy place, a dangerous place, or an evil place. And then I'll ask myself, *Is this really the kind of person I want to live with for the rest of my life? Are they working on being less of a victim, less of a controller? Are they using controlling tendencies for good causes (nursing, teaching, serving as a member of the clergy) or bad (manipulating, terrorizing, politicking)?*

I'm also going to use early childhood memories to understand a potential partner's rule book, asking myself, *Is this person's rule book compatible with mine?* By compatible, I don't mean the same—you'll never find that, and the same, as I've already stated, isn't always the best. What I mean by compatible is this: Sande is willing to live with the fact that I'm a bit of a rule breaker, and I appreciate the fact that Sande wouldn't break a rule if it was passed by a group of third graders. She brings order into my life; I bring a little fun into hers. Our rule books work well together, and neither Sande nor I ever try to change each other's rule book.

I'll also use early childhood memories to help correct previous bad choices. For instance, I think most of us, in our ideal moments, want to marry a giver. So then why do so many people, women in particular, marry a taker?

If this is your story, step back and ask yourself the hard questions. Go ahead—no one is listening. I can't even hear you. Be brutally honest. When you went with that last taker for three and a half years, what did it get you? Stress with your other family members who saw the guy for what he was? Lack of time with people who really care about you and aren't interested in just using you? A broken heart? An abortion?

Then have a conversation that goes something like this: *You know, I sort of gravitate toward those takers, don't I? I wonder why that is. You know what—my mom did that too. As much as I hate to admit it, I'm an awful lot like her. That's scary. She's gone through three marriages. I don't want to do that.*

This is smart-decision time: Are you going to behave differently in the future? Are you going to delve into your memories so you understand your basic motivation? Will you be directed by responsible choices or swept off your feet by the next taker who is just a little more handsome, a little slicker, and a little more packaged than the last taker?

If this is a trouble area for you, I suggest that you read my books *The Birth Order Connection* or *Women Who Try Too Hard.*

Don't get me wrong; takers can be fun—for a while. But eventually, especially if you marry one, you'll be left alone. He'll be out bow hunting or bowling when you're left home changing diapers. When you're gripped with menstrual cramps, he'll be at the corner bar with his buddies or sitting in a recliner asking when dinner is going to be ready. If you truly want to hunt for a giver, you need to stop acting like someone who is easily taken.

Finally, I'm going to look at this person's capability to speak my love language. If I need a lot of time, I'll be nothing but miserable if I marry a Type A person who will always be too busy to fulfill the needs of my love language. If one of my primary goals is to live in a nice neighborhood and send all my kids to a private school, I might want to marry someone who can love me by providing the financial income necessary for me to afford all that. I'll have to sacrifice some of this person's time, conversation, and attention, but that won't matter so much if my love language is receiving gifts (within reason).

I also have to realize that by marrying someone (or by having kids), I'm making a commitment to address their love language for the rest of my life. If I can't stand the thought of a thirty-minute heart-to-heart talk, why would I marry a person who will always want to be loved with words of affirmation or quality time?

When you look at a relationship this way, you're asking the kinds of questions that will lead to a truly compatible and lifelong union.

### Marrieds

Now what about if you're already married and haven't followed birth order, love languages, and the like? No need to get too nervous—yet! Once the choice is made, you need to make the best of it, and you can if you're armed with the right information. I know a number of happily married first borns, for instance, who have beaten the odds and who have a very successful relationship.

The main thing is to be aware of your weaknesses, anticipate the fallout, and learn to act accordingly. For instance, if two first borns are in my office, I'm going to warn them that they may fight more than other couples because both are used to being in charge. Both of them will need to learn to let the other person win now and then—even though doing so will feel like a completely foreign skill. I'll usually urge both partners to go out of their way to find different methods of serving their partner, rather than controlling or manipulating. I'll make full use of the love languages here, giving them an assignment to discover their partner's love language and then put it to full use.

With two last borns, I'll encourage them to watch their spending habits. They may need to write up a budget or maybe even visit a financial counselor. They'll have to learn to set a proper schedule for themselves and their children—even though doing so will seem constricting and weird. They'll also need to put the love languages to use, as both may be self-centered. The love languages will help them learn how to focus on someone else.

As a married man or woman, you can use temperaments to work through personal disagreements. If you're a melancholy, you can learn to lighten up—not everybody has to read the newspaper from front to back just because you think that's the right way to do it. Let your sanguine partner start with the comics or the sports page, and learn to choose your battles wisely.

If you're a choleric, understand that love is not about winning or doing things your way; it's about serving, cherishing others, and putting others first. If you're a phlegmatic, you need to do the opposite of what I'm suggesting the cholerics do—that is, you may have to assert yourself more and be more honest about your feelings and more forthright about your desires, or else you risk falling into a smoldering resentment when you never get your way.

Exploring your spouse's childhood memories, as well as your own, will help you understand why your husband has a naïve optimism or why your wife has taken years to start feeling safe in your relationship. You've married a person with a very influential past. For good or for ill, this past is part of your marriage, and it's perilous to ignore it. You can't rewrite your spouse's rule book—only he or she can do that, and only within certain parameters. What you can do is become more understanding of the mental processes your spouse goes through as he or she makes decisions and responds to others.

Your application of love languages should be obvious: Discovering a loved one's love language gives you the key to their heart. Learning to master the love languages will make you a well-rounded person who is thoughtful and considerate and a great friend, parent, and spouse. Ultimately you'll derive far more fulfillment from loving others well than even from being well loved yourself.

## Vocations

Everything we've talked about can be readily applied in the workplace. For example, a salesperson could improve her sales remarkably if she would start approaching potential customers by considering their birth order.[2] And you don't want to treat a first-born boss the same way you'd treat a last-born boss. The first-born boss will probably want just the facts; he needs data to support his conclusions, and if you come in with an emotional appeal, you'll lose nine times out of ten.

If you're trying to get through to a last born, however, you'll need to schmooze a little bit—but not in any way showing a lack of respect (last borns are sensitive to not being respected). If you can effectively use humor, so much the better. Make your time with the last born enjoyable, and you'll increase your effectiveness with her more often than not.

We don't have time to go through every scenario. I recommend you pick up my book *Winning the Rat Race without Becoming a Rat* for a more thorough discussion. For now, go back through the birth-order characteristics and ask yourself, *Given this person's disposition, what's the best way to interact with her?*

As you choose your vocation or consider a vocational change, put birth order to work for you. Most middle borns make excellent middle managers. They can be great assistant principals, but they may actually enjoy being an assistant principal more than becoming the senior principal. Protect yourself from being promoted to a position in which you won't be able to succeed.

Does this mean middle-born children are unfit to be CEOs and presidents? Of course not—I've already mentioned several past U.S. presidents who were middle-born children. Our personal history and makeup is too unique to develop hard and fast rules, but using all four of the personality predictors we've talked about in this book (birth order, temperament, early childhood memories, and love language) should give you an accurate self-understanding as well as a good idea of the types of jobs you'll be satisfied doing.

For example, while I know a successful accountant who is a last born, most last borns—particularly if they're sanguine by temperament—would be bored stiff as accountants. They need more interaction with people than the accounting profession usually provides.

Also consider your temperament. If you're a sanguine, you may need to think twice about being self-employed if self-employment will mean staying home by yourself and working in virtual isolation all day long. While some people revel in solitude (especially phlegmatics), others can't stand it.

Cholerics will have a difficult time taking orders from others. They usually won't enjoy a job that offers little personal freedom or that feels too constricting. Melancholies need time to think and reflect; sanguines usually prefer a more relaxed environment. Take all these factors into consideration when you think about where you can be most successful.

187

In addition to using temperament and birth order, use early childhood memories to increase your performance and to anticipate potential pitfalls. If your boss has a rule book in which rules are sacred just because they are rules, and your rule book states that rules are made to be broken, check your natural tendencies and do things by the book. You can drive five miles per hour over the speed limit as soon as you get out of the office, but you'd better not leave until the clock is firmly past 5:00. If your boss's rule book leads her to believe that the world is a scary place, you should go out of your way to show her you're not a threat—you're on her side.

If I keep messing up, I can use my memories to provide me with clues as to why. I can look at them with these questions lingering in my mind: Am I a bridge builder, or do I burn bridges? Do I burn bridges because I get mad when things don't go my way? Have I been too petty, too lazy, too irresponsible? Why might that be? And how can I change that?

If I want to show appreciation for my boss or coworkers or subordinates, I'll use love languages to recognize that different people value different methods of affirmation. For instance, during an evaluation I may offer several different bonuses for Christmas, maybe even letting people make their own choice: an extra day off, a new office chair, a round of golf, etc. If I know an employee is dying for words of affirmation, I'll put his name in the company newspaper and give him a big compliment. In other words, I won't treat everyone the same because I know they don't want to be affirmed in the same way.

## Getting to Know You More

I can hear the naysayers already. "Come off it, Leman. How am I supposed to know my boss's birth order without looking like an idiot? And for crying out loud—you must be joking when you talk about learning a subordinate's love language. That type of thinking would get me laughed out of the office."

Not so fast: There's a simple tool you can use that is remarkably effective to reveal all we've talked about and more. It's inexpensive but highly efficient. It's called "conversation."

I'm not suggesting you act like a shrink during a lunch or coffee break: "So, Susan, tell me three early childhood memories . . ." But you can intermingle comments with the group's analysis of the Buffalo Bills and Washington Redskins: "So, you went to the game with your brother? Is that an older brother, or younger?"

More often than not, the person you ask will usually give you his full birth order: "He's my older brother. There's just the two of us."

When the group gets together just to talk, listen for clues about rule books: Is one man always ridiculing the type of people who toe the party line? Is another woman upset because people don't obey the yellow "recommended" speed limit sign on the curve just a mile north of the office?

Pay attention to what people complain about. Do they feel overworked? Underappreciated? Undercompensated? You don't need to quiz someone to find out these things.

Temperament is pretty easy to pick up on if you just take a few minutes to think about the people you know. It doesn't take a doctorate to tell a sanguine from a melancholy—just listen to who laughs more! A choleric will be involved in most of the politicking, and the melancholy will love to pass out ten-page memos on the correct use of the copy machine, while the phlegmatic will try to help everyone just get along.

In short, I'm asking you to take a sincere interest in the people you work with. Get to know them. Find out what motivates them. Take your eyes off yourself for a few minutes and learn to look at the world through their eyes.

But while you do all this, can I add one other item? In addition to better understanding yourself and others, I hope this book has helped you to *appreciate* yourself more. You truly are unique, one of a kind, designed by no less skilled a creator than God himself. If the one who put the stars in place loves you just the way he designed you, how long is it going to take you to learn to love yourself?

With an accurate self-awareness, a considerate concern for others, and a healthy self-appreciation, you can go much further than you realize. But before we complete our time together, I want to offer a few more skills. In the next chapter, I want to teach you how to be your own shrink.

# 11

## Becoming Your Own Shrink

This chapter is where you really get your money's worth. Instead of dropping thousands of dollars on expensive therapy, for the few bucks this book costs I'll take you through the new beliefs, attitudes, and actions that will help you reshape your personality for the better. Along the way, we'll follow another individual who underwent real personal change. He happens to be one of my favorite actors: Steve Martin.

Before you can improve upon your personality, however, it's vital that you stop pretending. You won't have the energy to both create a false persona and improve your real persona. Eventually, you're going to have to choose: Do I really want to change, or do I want to keep pretending?

191

## The Real You

In 1990 Red Sox catcher John Marzano appeared during a casting call for the film *Other People's Money*. He quickly gathered a crowd by signing autographs and telling inside stories about what really happens in the Red Sox dugout and locker room. One particularly touching story included the account of outfielder Dwight Evans, who Marzano says cried on his shoulder the day he was released from Boston.

There's just one problem: John Marzano was never at that audition. He was impersonated by Kevin Winn, an aspiring actor who did a fairly good job of making his case—though understandably upsetting Marzano in the process.[1]

In 1999 Notre Dame all-American halfback Nick Eddy found out that William McMullen, a high school football coach in Rochester, Massachusetts, was passing himself off as Eddy. McMullen had been so successful in his claims that even his wife and kids thought he was the star halfback.

In 2000 Marlins pitcher Bill Jones spoke to a Florida grade school assembly. At first the faculty was delighted to have a celebrity give a pep talk, but they became suspicious when Jones couldn't answer relatively basic questions about the club. Upon further investigation, they discovered that the Marlins didn't even have a Bill Jones on their roster. Instead, they had been visited by an imposter, Christopher Camp.

My favorite story is about how Heisman Trophy winner Danny Wuerffel obtained a $16,000 line of credit at a New Jersey Home Depot. Several of the employees were thrilled to be working with a Heisman Trophy winner, but a couple workers became suspicious when they noticed that Wuerffel misspelled Destin, Florida, the town where he lives. Apparently that was a bigger clue than the fact that the man who applied for the credit was quite slender and black—and Wuerffel weighs 212 pounds and is white.

All of us have two choices: Build on who we are or pretend to be someone else. Of course, only the most enterprising will become so bold as to try to take on someone else's name and identity, but I've found that many of the people who come to me for counseling spend a good bit of their day constructing a fake personality.

Why would you want to be someone else, anyway? You are unique; you're like a snowflake. If you're spending all your time and energy trying to be something you're not, it's high time you stop pretending and start thanking God for the way he so miraculously and wonderfully made you. When you find yourself doubting that you truly are unique and special, ask for God's forgiveness and move forward with a new determination not to dump on yourself.

I'm not saying that self-improvement doesn't take work. As you'll see in just a moment, it takes a *lot* of work. But you're not alone in this process. Let's see how it was played out in the life of Steve Martin.

## A Wild and Crazy Guy

If you're over thirty, you probably remember Steve Martin best from his hit *Saturday Night Live* skit entitled "Two Wild and Crazy Guys." Along with Dan Aykroyd, Steve dressed in loud outfits, talked obnoxiously, and basically made himself a very loud nuisance—with hilarious results. One of Steve's early comedy albums pictured him with balloons on his head on one side of the album and an arrow running through his head on the other side. If it could get a laugh, Steve would give it try. He once skated across the stage of *The Tonight Show* wearing a King Tut outfit!

A clear sanguine, if ever there was one.

Not surprisingly, Steve is the younger of two children. He had a knack for performance early on: As young as five years old, Steve was memorizing Red Skelton shows and performing them during show-and-tell at school. As a teenager, Steve worked at Disneyland and Knott's Berry Farm. He was the consummate class clown and was soon earning his living writing for well-known comedians, including the Smothers Brothers, Sonny and Cher, and Dick Van Dyke.

In 1970 Martin decided to strike out on his own, performing stand-up comedy himself. His career took off six years later with *Saturday Night Live,* and a few years after that his smash movie *The Jerk* established him as one of the most popular comedy performers of his day.

Of all Steve's movies, my personal favorite is the 1986 movie *Three Amigos!* I've always thought that movie is worthy of five stars, and my family has watched it with me so many times I know almost the entire screenplay by heart. I can't tell you how thrilled I was to learn that *Three Amigos!* may be one of Martin's favorite films as well. He told one magazine that *Three Amigos!* is the rare film of his that he actually watched from start to finish and found himself "laughing his head off."[2]

It's interesting that throughout his life Martin has tried on wildly divergent personalities. If you were to slap the sanguine label on him and leave it at that, you'd be sadly mistaken. Though he was a class clown, Steve earned straight A's at Long Beach State College, planning to be a philosophy professor, of all things, but then dropped out of college to perform a stand-up routine of goofy gags and outrageous innuendo. He then went back to what one writer called his "Straight Arrow Period." Martin cut his hair short, shaved off his facial hair, and appeared on stage in a white three-piece suit. That didn't last long; Martin soon went back to an outrageously funny style that could best be described as bizarre, and there he hit his stride.

But following the megasuccess of *The Jerk*, Martin went serious again, starring in *Pennies from Heaven*, a very somber movie with a decidedly unhappy ending. While another string of comedies followed, Martin regularly retreated to more serious fare (such as *Grand Canyon* and *The Spanish Prisoner*). He wrote some critically praised plays, including *Picasso at the Lapin Agile*, as well as a novella entitled *Shopgirl*.

Those are the acts of a first born or a melancholy, not a last-born sanguine! While his outrageous acts fit the bill perfectly for a sanguine, Martin has always defied easy labeling. He lives in a somewhat peculiar L-shaped building in L.A. with no front windows, a dwelling that Martin calls "the house that says 'Go away.'"[3] This mixture of the outgoing sanguine personality with the aloof, introverted streak is best seen in Martin's business cards. He doesn't like to sign autographs and mingle with fans, so instead he has signed business cards that read, "This certifies that you have had a personal encounter with me and that you found me warm, polite, intelligent and funny."[4]

It seems to me that Martin has melancholy (perfectionistic) tendencies. He was once quoted as saying, "I [write] a little at a time. Sometimes it takes years to finish." He then displays his sanguine nature in the same quote: "I never want to think it's work. If I thought I had to do some writing work, I'd just about die." Affirming his sanguine quality again, Martin adds that comic acting comes naturally to him. "It's a wild gene," he says. "I guess I'm just a show-off."[5]

I hope you realize by now how beneficial it can be for you to become more aware of yourself, as Steve has. He recognizes that he wants to have fun. He doesn't want to think of writing as work, but he also realizes that he's about more than just having fun. He has a serious streak too. He's getting in touch with the blended temperaments we talked about earlier.

Martin's example shows us how a person can adapt his personality while still maintaining his true self.

Martin calls his play *Picasso at the Lapin Agile* a "turning point in my life. . . . I remember seeing it a year later and thinking, 'I am really proud of this.'"[6] His success at writing plays has freed him up to pursue such diverse projects as writing an essay on playing the banjo for *The Oxford American* and an essay about a painter for *Art News*.

Part of this growth has to do with maturity. Martin explains, "I remember when I was younger, people would say something like, 'I don't care what they think.' I'd go: 'What do you mean by that? Because *I* care what they think.' And then you always hear older people say, 'I don't care what they think,' and you think, 'Yeah, you can do that when you get older.' And I started to understand that. You do start to not care what they think anymore. But you have to come to that. You have to go through a transition."[7]

Comics are passionately concerned about how others respond—their career depends on it. For Martin to confess that he cares less what others think is truly an impressive development. The class clown *can* cool off when it's appropriate to do so.

One of the more profound influences on Steve's life was when his father and then two close friends all died within a couple years of each other. During the same stretch, Steve also suffered a painful and somewhat messy divorce. Maybe similar circumstances in your own life led you to pick up this book. A close friend died, you lost your job, a parent passed away, or a major life event occurred that shook you up and led you to begin thinking, perhaps for the very first time, about how you'll be remembered and what your priorities really are in life—and whether, like Scrooge on Christmas Eve, you have time to change.

In response to these pressures, Martin says, "[I] sort of changed myself, psychologically and professionally. I looked at what I was doing and I wasn't that fulfilled—in the movies. In the writing world I was very happy. In fact that kind of saved me emotionally, the fact I had *something* that I could be proud of."[8]

Martin took three years off and decided to work on his personality. Friends noticed a difference. "I think he got more open," director Frank Oz states. "He's become a warmer individual and more layered. I think he's become more wine than grape juice, which is a good thing."[9]

Isn't that a powerful statement? Wouldn't you like one of your friends to see such a maturing that they might say, "Yeah, Susan has become more wine than grape juice"? Brian Grazer, a Hollywood producer, used to put up with Steve calling and saying, "Let's talk," but then hearing him say, fifteen or thirty seconds later, "Okay, seeyalater!"[10]

That type of attitude is grape juice.

Now Steve has decided to hold a certain number of dinner parties every week with a rotating circle of friends, purposefully creating a more social life for himself and going out of his way to invite non-Hollywood types to broaden his experience and his personality.

That type of attitude is wine.

Now in his mid-fifties, Steve has an opportunity to reevaluate how he has lived. "I wish I had paid as much attention to my personal life as I did to my professional life," he told one writer. "I didn't know how, but that's changing. The only regret I have is that I didn't learn things faster in life. I recently sat next to a woman who was in her 80s, and she said, 'Well, finally, you've become wise, and it's not too late.'"[11]

The key here is to see Steve Martin as a work in progress. He recognized some weaknesses in his life—superficiality in relationships, for example—and decided to make a change. Without losing his natural sense of humor—a true, priceless gift if ever there was one—Steve has deepened himself to also become known as "wise" by his friends.

## Personality Makeover

Let's look at how you too can begin to work on such a personality makeover.

### Step One: Look Back

People come to my office because they want a different future:

"Dr. Leman, I want to find a husband who will respect me!"

"Dr. Leman, I want my child to succeed!"

"Dr. Leman, I want to stop stuffing my face with food!"

While I appreciate the fact that they know just what they want, I have to frustrate them a little bit by calling a time-out and saying, "Before we look forward, let's take a look back."

Of course you're concerned about the future. That's why you bought this book. But the only way you can positively impact your future is to make better choices by becoming more aware of your past.

That's what I did my senior year in high school. All my classmates were talking about going to college and university. While they were excited about their plans, I found myself becoming very sad. It suddenly dawned on me that this wonderful little family of people in a small town wouldn't spend the rest of their lives hanging out at Jack's hotdog stand on Friday nights. "You mean I won't see Jim the dork walk around with ketchup on the corner of his mouth all night, oblivious to the fact that everybody saw what he didn't?" I asked myself one day. "You mean Sandy won't always stand outside Gordy's car, wearing her pink cashmere sweater and flipping that beautiful mane of golden hair? You mean Moonhead and I won't keep giving John wedgies and making everybody laugh by running little Dickie's underwear up the school flagpole? All that is gonna stop?"

Suddenly, the thought occurred to me, *I've been a fool. I've spent four years in high school entertaining my classmates, largely because of my own insecurities, but what have all those antics gotten me? Nothing. My friends are getting ready to build a future, and I'm looking into the frightening reality of classic underachievement.*

I can't tell you how important it was that I looked back at where my past actions had gotten me—and why. If all I had done was look ahead—who could I entertain the next year?—I would have been like Charlie Brown, who really did believe that this time it would be different. This time Lucy wouldn't pull the football away from him just before he kicked it. Based on the past, Charlie had no reason to believe anything Lucy told him, but Charlie never looked back. He only looked forward and fell on his backside every single time.

Once I took an honest (and painful) look back, I was willing to admit I had to do some things differently. Thank God for that schoolteacher, Miss Wilson. She showed me that maybe I could use those off-the-wall, comical antics to do good someday.

She was right. I believe that one of the reasons I frequently have standing-room-only attendance in my seminars is that I'm driven to make sure everyone is having fun. That does wonders for word-of-mouth publicity.

This philosophy covers just about everything I do. For instance, I recently appeared on a nationally syndicated radio show that most authors drool over, though few get invited. The reason so many writers want to be on this show is that just one appearance can make your book sales take off. Appearing two days in a row is a dream. But the producers booked me for three full programs. Why? Well, I must have had something to say, but I think it also comes back to the fact that they have a good time when I'm on the air. Whenever I appear on *The View* or the *Today* show, my gauge of success isn't, "What did the host think?" but rather, "Did I get the camera crew to laugh?" If the production people are holding their sides, I'm thinking, *This is working!* and I know I'm going to be invited back.

The key is to look back and understand the basic strengths you bring to life and then figure out how to put them to better use and use them for different purposes. I am still the class clown, but now I've learned to use that skill to succeed in life rather than to get myself in trouble.

Steve Martin was always a person of depth, but he realized as a last-born sanguine that he was also naturally funny and able to write comedy. Even a comedic writer is still a writer, and Martin chose to build on that to create a new career as a novelist and essayist as well as an actor.

In short, Steve has not allowed himself to be boxed in. He has looked back, built on his strengths, and then continued to stretch himself and develop his personality, capitalizing on his history to create an even more promising future. You can do the same.

### Step Two: Take Small Steps

Next to *Three Amigos!* my favorite five-star movie is *What about Bob?* In this classic comedy, Leo Marvin (played by Richard Dreyfuss) has just written a smash best-seller entitled *Baby Steps*, when he runs into the neurotic of all neurotics, Bob (played by Bill Murray).

One of the humorous things about this movie is how they make fun of a book title that actually makes very good sense: Mental health and personal change are both best pursued through baby steps. Some people become intent on making a change but then go about it in the wrong way. Instead of working steadily toward progress, they seek to make colossal jumps, which virtually guarantees failure. Then they say, "See, I knew I would fail; I shouldn't even try."

Whenever someone asks me, "How am I going to do things differently?" I answer, "By making many different choices." They're looking for a silver bullet; I'm trying to show them they need an entire arsenal.

Few strategies work once and for all. Our brains just don't operate that way. I was twenty-two years old when I quit smoking, but three decades later, I can still remember how good a cigarette tastes after a meal. I don't crave cigarettes anymore, but that habit has probably shaped me for life.

The crux behind any behavioral change is first looking back and admitting that what you've been doing in the past hasn't worked—that's what we covered in step one—and then making many small changes to go someplace different.

For example, let's take a woman who's a classic pleaser. This woman says "yes" even when she means "no"; she lets other people virtually run her life, and whenever anything goes wrong she immediately accepts the blame, even if it wasn't her fault. She can't bear to disappoint anyone, which makes her miserable, as she leaves no time for herself and consents to a schedule that runs her ragged.

There's no magic bullet for a woman like this. Instead, I tell her in no uncertain terms, "June, you have to realize that saying 'yes' when you mean 'no' needs to stop—beginning today." Then I teach her how to say no; without this skill, change will never happen. Pleasers are worried first and foremost about offending others, so their "no" is usually pretty wishy-washy. June needs to find a different way to communicate.

"After you've been asked to do something that you know you shouldn't do, I want you to start your statement with the word 'No.' Got that? The first word out of your mouth has to be 'No,' as in 'No, I'm unable to help you.'

"When Patricia from the PTA starts talking about how good you are at running the carnival, you don't say, 'Well,

Patricia, I'd really like to help, but. . . .' Instead, you say, 'No, Patricia, I'm unable to help this year.' And whatever you do, don't give any excuses."

"But why, Dr. Leman?"

"Because when you give an excuse—'I'd like to help, but Jack is working overtime, and our daughter has started dance and has lots of recitals, and I just don't have the time to run the entire carnival'—you give Patricia time to say, 'What if I got Lisa to help you out this year? She's so good at decorating and managing her time.' Patricia can yank on your pleaser's strings like a master martinet operator, and before long you'll feel like a helpless puppet who has just agreed to do one more thing you don't have time to do.

"Cut all that out. Simply say, 'No, I'm unable to help this year.'"

Now before June can claim victory, she's going to have to repeat this process many times. She doesn't stop being a pleaser with one visit to my office. She has to learn, through a series of baby steps, how to say no. If she's really neck-deep in being a pleaser, she may even have to begin by picking and choosing who she stands up to. For instance, instead of her mother-in-law, she might practice saying no to a telemarketer on the phone. The important thing is that she recognizes that change is a long process. Though I haven't read the book, I came across a title that I think makes so much sense: *A Long Obedience in the Same Direction*. That sounds like a pretty successful formula to me.

A friend of mine has suffered with depression throughout most of his adult life. I was near his hometown while on a business trip and decided to stop by to see him. My visit was personal. I was just being his friend, not his shrink. As soon as he opened the door, I knew he needed help. He must have had three or four days' growth of beard on his face.

"Jim, are you growing a beard?" I asked later, after we had caught up on each other's life.

"No," Jim responded in a very slow, depressed tone.

"Can I give you a simple suggestion, just as a friend?"

"Sure."

"Tomorrow morning when you get up, shave."

It may sound stupid and trite for me to offer such basic advice, but all this goes back to baby steps; even when you're depressed, and you don't feel like shaving or washing your hair or taking a shower, sometimes you still need to force yourself to do those mundane things. Over time those seemingly mundane tasks become profound steps toward long-term personality change.

This same principle holds true whether you're trying to curb destructive eating habits, inappropriate sexual behavior, or any personality trait you want changed. If you know you talk too much at dinner, decide that the next time you eat with a group of people, you'll try to cut down your talking by 25 percent. Force yourself to be quiet, to listen, and to pay attention to others.

Practice may not make us perfect, but if you believe in the magic bullet, you might as well believe in the tooth fairy—both will get you the same thing (nothing!).

### Step Three: Improve Your Self-Talk

In that five-star movie *Three Amigos!* there's a hilarious scene in which Steve Martin's character finds himself in a terrible predicament. He goads himself on by repeating, "Gonna make it, gonna make it, gonna make it," but then gets slammed back against the wall every time.

Life can be like that sometimes, can't it? You think you're just about there—you've lost eight pounds and are really trying to eat better, when you're invited to your niece's wedding. That day, you eat particularly light—one small bowl of oatmeal for breakfast and a salad for lunch. Since

203

you've been doing so well, you give yourself permission to have one little piece of cake. Fifteen minutes later, you've had three pieces, so you say, "I've already blown it, so what the heck? I might as well have a fourth piece."

Basic human psychology means you have to learn to talk yourself through times of failure. Setbacks are going to come. It's not a matter of if, it's a matter of when. Have you developed the skills to talk yourself through?

For example, a woman trapped in a cycle of failure would say to herself, "I've blown it. Three pieces! How could I be so stupid? I'll always be fat. Well, if I'm going to be fat, one more piece of cake won't make any difference. In fact, another piece of cake might make me feel better."

A woman who learns the skills I'm talking about would say instead, "Okay, I probably shouldn't have had that second piece, and yes, a third piece sounds even better. But I've been doing very well, and I've worked very hard. Two pieces won't kill me. I don't want to eat a third, however, because that's the type of thing I did when I was losing control. I need to walk away from this table and find someone to talk to. Oh, there's Martha. She's always an encouraging person. I think I'll go walk over there, away from this table."

Let me be honest with you: This isn't just theory to me. I've had to live it out in my own life. One of my favorite pastimes is eating pumpkin pie. One morning, in preparation for hosting a little get-together later that evening, Sande asked me to stop by our local Marie Callenders and pick up two pies: one pumpkin and one lemon meringue. When I arrived at the store, I discovered that they had a special on pumpkin pies, so I decided to buy two pumpkin pies and one lemon meringue.

When I got home, the house was empty. It was 11:00 A.M. and I hadn't had time for breakfast that morning. Well, I looked down at the table and realized I had an extra pumpkin pie just sitting there. A piece of that pie with a little whipped cream would taste great with a cup of coffee.

I cut a generous slice and held it in my hand instead of using a fork. That was my first mistake. I ate it by chomping on it, not by tasting it. Boy, that first piece went down too easily, too quickly. Somehow my brain hadn't registered that I'd already eaten one rather generous piece of pumpkin pie. Besides that, my taste buds were going wild. That pie wasn't just good—it was near perfection.

I was thinking, *You know, that sucker was so good, and it brings the best out of my cup of coffee. I might just do an encore.*

Time for act two. I cut another piece, this one slightly larger. After all, no use selling myself short! The second piece went down just as easily as the first. I looked at the pie, three-eighths of which was gone, but I still had more coffee to drink and nothing to go with it.

*I'll take just one more one-inch slice to help me finish off my coffee,* I thought, but an inch slice of pie is like finger food. One direct hit to the tongue and it's gone. I did that several times until two-thirds of the pie had disappeared.

Now I've got a heck of a dilemma; my brain was finally catching up to my stomach, screaming out, "Overload! Overload!" But I've got another problem. Sande will be home shortly and she'll see that there's no one here but me! What do I tell her? The pie thief stopped at our house and ate over half the pie?

*Uh oh,* my conscientious self said. *I overdid it.*

*You know, Leman, there's a way around this,* my alter ego said.

*What's that?*

*Eat the evidence.*

I found the logic compelling. With one simple slice of the knife, I divided what was left of the pie into two pieces and wolfed both of them down. To my credit, I didn't put any whipped cream on the last several pieces.

In short, I ate the whole pie. I could hardly move, but I knew I was committed now and had to destroy all evidence, including the little foil pie tin, so I got up and stashed that in the bottom of the trash.

I sat down for a while, paying dearly for my choices, until Sande walked through the front door about twenty minutes later.

"Hi, honey," she said. "Did you get the pies?"

"Yeah, sure. They're on the counter."

"I'm going to make a fresh pot of coffee. Would you like a cup?"

"Sure."

Then Sande yelled from the kitchen. "This pie smells so good and would taste so delicious with your cup of coffee. Would you like me to cut you a slice?"

"Oh, no, honey," I said, my stomach bursting against its skin, "I gotta really start watching what I eat."

I'm just as weak as you are, only I may have bigger and worse failures. I've had to learn to make the little choices, just like you do.

Most of my practice is spent helping people to think and then to change their personal language. Instead of letting things happen, pause for a moment, think through what is taking place, and then self-talk your way out of it. When people face personality ruts and addictions, most often they're simply reacting—they hit upon a stimulus (delicious wedding cake or fabulous pumpkin pie) and let the collapse happen without using their brain as the powerful tool it can be.

I like to use phrases that shock people into seeing truth in a new way. One of those phrases is, "Don't just do something—stand there!" The cliché, of course, is just the opposite: "Don't just stand there, do something!" But if you're facing a personality rut, you need to pull back from the action and carefully talk your way through your next several steps.

Another good strategy behind positive self-talk is continually reminding yourself that even if you're not losing weight, you have other good things going on: your family, your spiritual life, your vocation, etc. In fact, if we think about it, most of us have at least seven different lives: our physical life, our emotional life, our relational life, our financial life, our spiritual life, our vocational life, and our family life. While three or even four of these lives may be very difficult for us at any one time, there is usually at least one or two lives that bring pleasure to us and on which we can focus. Your job might be getting you down, but you're really enjoying that after-work aerobics class. Your marriage might be going through a tough time, but that new Bible study you've been attending is a real pick-me-up. Your key to mental health is determining what lives you choose to focus on. There will always be one that isn't going perfectly; mentally healthy people learn to keep perspective by thinking about those things that lift them up and give them hope.

Keep in mind, this is a very freeing concept. Guess who gets to choose what life to focus on? That's right—you and no one else. People can hurt you, but they can't think for you. They can't shape where you place your focus, meaning you no longer have to be a slave to what anyone does to you.

### Step Four: Marshal Your Imaginative Energy

A woman who wanted to lose weight was somewhat offended by my suggestion. "You really want to lose weight?" I asked her.

"Of course I do," she said. "That's why I'm here."

I handed her a blank three-by-five card. "There you go," I said. "That's your key."

She looked at me like I had an arrow through my head. "What am I supposed to do with this?"

207

"I want you to write your current weight on it, date it, and then post it on your refrigerator door. It'll read like this: On January 25, 2002, my weight is 205."

"But everybody can see it there!"

"Exactly!" I said. "That's the point." Now she thought I was really crazy. "And while you're at it, why don't you take a second card? You can post this one on your desk at work."

Not everyone takes me up on this, but those who do find it to be tremendously beneficial. They're worried about being embarrassed, but can I be honest with you? If you weigh over two hundred pounds, everybody already knows it. Your weight is no secret, and frankly, whether they put you at 225 or 215, do you think it really matters to them? Probably not. But it matters to you, and when you publicly post your weight you're beginning to marshal the power of your imaginative energy. Most people spend half the day denying their problems. When you put your problem right in front of you, denial is shattered and you're finally able to do something about it.

I do this myself. When I went to the doctor, he took my vitals and sighed.

"What is it, doc?" I asked.

"Dr. Leman, your blood pressure is getting dangerously high. I'm afraid you're going to have to start watching what you eat."

Being in my late fifties, with a daughter who has yet to reach her teens, I'd kinda like to hang around a little longer, if for no other reason than to give the man who wants to marry Lauren a really hard time when he comes to ask me for her hand. Since Lauren has three older sisters, I figure I'll have lots of practice by then and can really give the guy a memory or two. For this and other reasons, I have ample motivation to truly care about the state of my blood pressure.

The problem is, blood pressure isn't an immediate pull; it's the type of thing I know I should address someday. And when I leave my office in the middle of the afternoon and feel my stomach start churning, and then pass an Arby's restaurant with a big sign advertising its bacon double-cheese cordon-bleu sandwich, well, *that's* immediate pressure. It's like my car is steering itself right into the drive through.

I took one of my doctor's cards, flipped it over, and wrote my blood pressure on it. I then taped it to my dashboard. Every morning that number is one of the first things I see. At lunchtime I see those numbers again. After work, on my way home, they're staring me in the face, helping me to drive past Arby's and go home and get a bowl of cereal with skim milk instead of the bacon double-cheese cordon-bleu sandwich. The cereal can hold me until dinner.

The thing I like about this exercise is that it not only marshals my imaginative energy, it also marshals the energy of my family and friends. When an associate drives with me to lunch, he'll invariably comment on that card. "What the heck is that?"

"My blood pressure."

"Sheesh, Cubby, you better lay off the peanut butter!"

"I know. That's why I put the card there."

So when we get into the restaurant and I start to look at the wrong part of the menu, my associate, my wife, or one of my kids will often smile, repeat the number, and point me toward the salads and low-fat alternatives.

These cards are just simple tools that remind you of where you want to go. They show you're serious about changing. If your problem is your temper, you might write out a Bible verse: "Better a patient man than a warrior, a man who controls his temper than one who takes a city" (Prov. 16:32). That way, if you lose it, your friends and family can smile, point to the refrigerator, and say, "Proverbs 16:32," and you know exactly what they're talking about.

If your kids have decided they want to remain virgins until their wedding night (and I hope they have), they can post a card on their dresser mirror or car dashboard: "I'm worth waiting for." If a guy ever gets in her car or bedroom, he'll immediately know your child's goals—waiting until marriage.

Most of the families who come into my office or who ask me questions during seminars or radio programs have no port of call. That is, they don't have a safe harbor to run to or a strategy for beating back life's inevitable pressures and temptations. Consequently, when the waves hit, many capsize. While I've never run a marathon myself (if I ever want to feel that kind of pain, I'll simply ask one of my kids to hit me repeatedly with a two-by-four and save myself the blisters), I've talked to people who have, and the successful ones all say the same thing: "You better begin the race with some strategies if you want to complete it." You have to think about the moments of decision ahead of time—what you'll do if you feel tired at ten miles, how you'll respond if you feel you're slipping behind your pace and feeling unusually tired at eighteen miles, etc.

A young man who won his state's high school championship race in the mile impressed his coach with the way he marshaled his imaginative energy. "If I get boxed out in the first lap, this is what I'm going to do," he told his coach on the way to the meet. "I'll work my way to the outside, but make sure I look over my shoulder so I don't trip. If the pace is slow, I'm going to take the lead. If it's too fast, I'm going to hold back but still maintain contact. By the third lap, I want to be right on Rob Waller's heels. . . ."

He used his imaginative energy to think about every potential problem so that when it arose he'd know exactly what to do. If you want to change yourself, you need to use this same power. Marshal your imaginative energy.

Let's go back to the woman who wanted to lose weight. In addition to publicly posting her numbers, I helped her develop some strategies.

"You know yourself, Eileen; you know your downfall. What is it that really puts on the weight? What's your favorite treat at night?"

"That's easy. Breyer's mint chocolate chip ice cream with chocolate sauce."

"Who brings the ice cream home?"

"I do."

"So what do you think is a good strategy?"

"Not buying the ice cream in the first place."

"That's an improvement, but what will you do when the ice cream craving hits?" See, I know this stuff, because I've lived it too.

Eileen smiled. "Probably go out and buy some."

"Of course you will. Tell me, do you like sherbet?"

"Yeah, but not as much as ice cream."

"Me neither. But why don't you try buying a pint container of sherbet the next time you're at the grocery store? Instead of going completely cold turkey, when you get the ice cream craving you can give yourself a small single scoop of sherbet. And let's see if we can't make that pint of sherbet last at least seven to ten days, okay?"

Let me tell you—if Eileen can substitute a half-gallon of ice cream with a pint of sherbet, she will have made great progress. But to get there, she'll have to devise a strategy ahead of time. She'll have to marshal her imaginative energy.

### Step Five: Know Your Destination

In addition to knowing your problem (overtalkativeness, impatience, gossip, etc.), you need to know your solution. When my doctor told me what was wrong with my blood pressure numbers, he gave me better numbers to shoot for. If I want to lose a few pounds, I not only want to know where I am now but where I hope to be in two or three months.

The best way to treat a vice is to plant an opposing virtue. One of my daughters found herself caught up in an ugly, middle school game—gossip. Gossip can be a disease among teenage girls, and it can spread like liquid butter on a hot piece of toast. My daughter found herself joining in, but one night she confessed how guilty it made her feel.

"Daddy, I know it's wrong to talk bad about someone behind their back, but sometimes it seems like I can't help myself. I want to join in the talk and be a part of the group. What else can I do?"

My daughter wasn't dumb. She knew that if everyone always gossiped about everybody else, it was only a matter of time until she herself got slammed—if she hadn't already. Plus, it made her feel miserable the next time she saw one of the girls who had been gossiped about.

I could have given a sanctimonious talk about how she could confront her friends and say, "Gossip is a sin! Gossip is evil!" But I don't think that would have taken her very far. Instead, I asked, "Honey, why don't you be different?"

Unfortunately, different is not a word that middle school–age girls cherish, so I added, "Would you be willing to try a little experiment? I don't want you to feel guilty, and I think this will help you make even more friends."

"Okay, Daddy."

"Try planting a virtue wherever there's a vice."

"How do I do that?"

"What's the opposite of gossip?"

"I'm not sure."

"Well, if you heard someone talking about you, would you want to hear negative things or positive things?"

"Positive, I guess."

"Sure you would. So here's what I want you to do. Why don't you talk to Megan about Shawna, but get Megan to say something positive. Bait her: 'Megan, don't you think Shawna has pretty hair?' That type of thing. Megan will agree with you if you keep giving her opportunities. Then your job is to go to Shawna and say, 'I heard Megan talking about you this morning.' 'Oh yeah?' Shawna will ask. 'What did she say?' At first Shawna will be suspicious, thinking it's something negative, but you'll get to surprise her by saying, 'She was telling me how sweet you are and how much she loves that outfit you wore yesterday.' Then Shawna will probably compliment Megan right back."

"How do you know?"

"I'm a psychologist, honey, trust me. She'll say something like, 'Shawna is so encouraging. I just love that new haircut she got last week,' and you know what you'll do next, right?"

"I'll tell Megan what Shawna said?"

"That's right! Do that with the worst gossips. Help them feel how wonderful it is to discover encouragement instead of gossip."

My daughter went to her classmates and put this experiment to work. It was an unqualified success. While there were still occasional gab sessions, overall the friends took a big step toward encouragement rather than character assassination.

You can do the same thing. Instead of simply telling yourself, "I don't want to yell at the kids," figure out a positive response: "I'm going to set firm guidelines. If the guidelines aren't followed, I won't yell. Instead, I'll calmly inform them of the consequences, which they were told about ahead of time. There will be no discussion and no argument—just clear guidelines and clear consequences."

If a man comes to me struggling with pornography, one of my first aims is to get him to put the same amount of energy, time, and money into his romantic relationship with his wife that he used to spend on porn. "Why don't you take all the money you'll save from not calling 1-900 numbers and bring home some flowers for your wife, completely unexpected? Instead of spending an evening in a strip club, why don't you arrange to have a baby-sitter and take your wife to a nice hotel?"

Men who carry on "extracurricular" activities have to plan how to cover their tracks, and the sex industry isn't cheap. Men can drop hundreds of dollars a month on this addiction. They complain that their wife isn't interested, but if they would spend the same amount of time planning a romantic evening for her as they do planning an excuse to get away surreptitiously, they might find that the climate at home would change.

If you're too harsh with your kids, focus on becoming gentler. If you talk too much in a group, focus on becoming a good listener. If you are too shy, plan to introduce yourself to at least three people you've never met at the next party.

In short, know where you want to go, and take small steps to get there.

### Step Six: Give Yourself Room to Fail

Ichiro Suzuki made headlines around the world in 2001 when he became the first position player from Japan to win a full-time spot with a major league baseball team (the Seattle Mariners). The headlines kept coming when Ichiro hit an astonishing .360 his first two months of the season, at that point having the second highest batting average of anyone in the American league!

But think about this: What does a .360 batting average mean? It means that Ichiro gets a hit roughly one out of three times—a little more than that, but not much. Almost no one gets a hit four out of ten times over the course of a season, which means baseball greatly reveres people who fail at the plate roughly two-thirds of the time.

The all-or-none theory—I'll quit once for all—rarely works. When someone lives by this philosophy, what often happens is that they quit smoking successfully for a couple weeks, then the roof falls in—financial pressure, a smart-mouthed kid, a tough time at work—and in near desperation, they light up a cigarette. The person who lives by the all-or-none theory thinks, "Well, I blew it. I had a cigarette, I ruined the whole thing, so I might as well go back to smoking."

I'm suggesting you have an entirely different response. Encourage yourself with these words: "I went two weeks without a cigarette! I wish I could have gone two months, but two weeks is a good start. Though I messed up today, tomorrow's a new day, and I'll do better then."

A baseball player doesn't quit trying after one strikeout or even a series of strikeouts. In fact, it's not uncommon for players having a great year to go through occasional slumps. In the first year of his famous $25-million-a-year contract, Texas Ranger Alex Rodriguez Jr. was having a sensational season. He led the American League in home runs, was right up there for RBIs (runs batted in), and had a very respectable .333 batting average. But during one series with his former team, A. Rod batted 1–10, or .100. That means he created an out nine times out of ten! Nobody thought he should quit. Nobody said, "He's lost it." Baseball teaches us to handle failure and move on. So does life.

Remember baby steps? That's what you need. Ever see a baby walk? They go backwards sometimes, don't they? We will too. One flub doesn't mean the entire program is wrecked; it just means we're human and we need to recollect our strength to give it one more go.

## Finally—Someone with a Vision

Apparently Steve Martin picked up a lot of this stuff on his own. His biographer, Morris Walker, writes:

But just as Steve has blasted into the galaxy of stars, he is imploding into the microcosm. The bigger he gets, he still manages to "get small." It's interesting to note that since Steve made it big, his personal letterhead had a simple Helvetica type face at the top of the page, which read "Steve Martin" in clear, embossed, capital letters. Then, around 1990, Steve's traditional letterhead changed. He still had that same simple "STEVE MARTIN" at the top of his beige linen stationery that he used for 25 years, but this new letter I received had a new phrase:

STEVE MARTIN
"Finally, someone with a vision"

. . . Anyone who ever worked with Steve, saw him perform, or watched him attempt to do anything he set his mind to was keenly aware of Steve's vision. It's tunnel vision. But as I've mentioned many times in these pages, Steve is a very private person. His tunnel vision is an obvious manifestation of his aspirations. It's the method by which he accomplishes anything and everything . . . The distant light at the end is only a glimmer to even the greatest visionary. Only Steve sees his visions as they will one day exist.[12]

All of us can have this same vision, building on what we are, toward what we are not yet. It will take time, maturity, and sometimes supernatural help, but eventually we can become the type of person we've dreamed about becoming.

## Rehearsed Grace

The name Fred Astaire has become synonymous with grace, charm, and dancing ability. While Fred was certainly graceful, wonderfully charming, and perhaps one of the best dancers ever to come out of Hollywood, the truth is, he wasn't born that way—he worked at it, and he worked hard.

A friend of Astaire's told a magazine editor about how one day before an Academy Awards ceremony in which he was scheduled to receive a lifetime achievement Oscar, Fred spent the better part of an afternoon practicing getting out of his seat and bounding up the stairs onto the stage to receive his award. Onlookers were amazed to see a man spend so much time rehearsing such a simple procedure.

The night of the awards ceremony, millions of viewers saw a very gifted dancer seemingly glide effortlessly up those steps; what they never saw was the practice that went into the creation of such a "natural" effort.[13]

Your personality can be practiced in the same way. At first, patience may not come naturally to you. You might be more inclined to gossip than to encourage. You might have a difficult time holding back from talking about yourself, or you might be too shy or too aggressive. But if you practice like Fred did, if you put the principles we've already talked about into play, eventually you can create the best version of you.

As flawed and imperfect as you are, you can move forward in life. If there's a sense of realness about you, others will seek you out and sometimes even ask your counsel. When this starts happening, you'll know you've arrived at a special place. You've understood who you are, and you'll stand ready to achieve your full potential.

# Notes

## Chapter 1 The Personality Makeover

1. Peter Johnson, "Gumbel's Guffaw," *USA Today*, 8 November 1999, D5.

## Chapter 2 Many People, Four Flavors

1. Based on the overviews provided in the appendix of Marita Littauer, *Love Extravagantly* (Minneapolis: Bethany, 2001) and on Marita Littauer and Betty Southard, *Come as You Are* (Minneapolis: Bethany, 1999).

2. Florence Littauer, *Personality Plus* (Grand Rapids: Revell, 1983), 14.

## Chapter 4 Making the Most of Who You Are

1. Tim Crothers, "Is Youth Served?" *Sports Illustrated*, 18 June 2001, 28.

2. Quotes and information about Will Rogers have been taken from the following sources: Donald Day, ed., *The Autobiography of Will Rogers* (Boston: Houghton Mifflin, 1949); Eddie Cantor, "The Uncommon Will Rogers," *Great Lives, Great Deeds* (Pleasantville, NY: Reader's Digest Association, 1964); Homer Croy, *Our Will Rogers* (Boston: Little, Brown & Co., 1953).

3. Quotes on Charlton Heston are taken from Charlton Heston, *The Actor's Life: Journals 1956–1976* (New York: E.P. Dutton, 1976) and John Richardson, "Heston," *Esquire*, July 2001.

4. Quotes and information about Oprah Winfrey are taken from the following sources: Deirdre Donahue, "Live Your Best Life, with Oprah," *USA Today*, 2 July 2001, 1D; Joanna Powell, "Oprah's Awakening," *Good Housekeeping*, December 1998, 209; Oprah Winfrey, "The Courage to Dream," *Essence*, December 1998, 149; "Oprah Encourages Roosevelt University Grads . . ." *Jet*, 19 June 2000; Lisa Russell and Cindy Dampier, "Oprah Winfrey," *People*, 15 March 1999, 22; Ron Stodghill, "Daring to Go There," *Time*, 5 October 1998, 80; Lynette Clemetson, "Oprah on Oprah," *Newsweek*, 8 January 2001, 41; Maya Angelou, "How Oprah's Changed Our World," *McCall's*, November 1998, 67; Emma Bland, "Battle of the Bulge," *McCall's*, November 1998, 68; Lynette Clemetson, "It Is a Constant Work," *Newsweek*, 8 January 2001, 45.

5. Quotes and information about Tiger Woods are taken from the following sources: Gannett News Service, "No Heroics for Tiger," *Bellingham Herald,* 18 June 2001, 83; "Tiger Woods," *Headliners and Legends with Matt Lauer,* Friday 15 June 2001, NBC; Christine Brennan, "Storm Is Merciful to Tiger," *USA Today,* 15 June 2001, 14C; Dan Jenkins, "A Slam by Any Name," *Golf Digest,* June 2001, 180.

6. Quotes and information about Jay Leno and Dave Letterman are taken from the following sources: Bill Carter, *The Late Shift: Letterman, Leno, and the Network Battle for the Night* (New York: Hyperion, 1994); Lloyd Grove, "Late-Night Sweats," *Vanity Fair,* October 1996, 176; Bill Zehme, "Letterman Lets His Guard Down," *Esquire,* December 1994, 98; James Wolcott, "Letterman Unbound," *The New Yorker,* 3 June 1996, 82; David Handelman, "Dave's Real World," *Vogue,* January 1995, 78; Fred Schruers, "Dave vs. Dave," *Rolling Stone,* 30 May 1996, 30; Tom Gliatto, "Fade to Black," *People,* 26 October 1998.

7. Quotes and information about Anne Morrow Lindbergh are taken from Dorothy Herrmann, *Anne Morrow Lindbergh: A Gift for Life* (New York: Ticknor and Fields, 1993), 2, 9, 38, 42, 45–46, and Gary Thomas, *Sacred Marriage* (Grand Rapids: Zondervan, 2000).

## Chapter 5 Making Sense of Birth Order

1. David Hill, *The New Century Bible Commentary: The Gospel of Matthew* (Grand Rapids: Eerdmans, 1972), 131.

## Chapter 6 The Little Boy or Girl You Once Were, You Still Are

1. Michael Bamberger, "Dom DiMaggio," *Sports Illustrated,* 2 July 2001, 105.

2. Ibid., 106.

3. Cited in Dan Vergano, "Mind Makes Memories Fonder—but False," *USA Today,* 2 July 2001, 1D.

4. Ibid.

5. Ibid.

6. Ibid.

## Chapter 7 Your Rule Book

1. These and other details are taken from Mark Seal, "Still Afloat," *Golf Digest,* August 2001, 99.

2. Ibid., 108.

## Chapter 8 Is Life Working Out for You?

1. Andy Seiler, "Lemmon Was Just One of Us," *USA Today,* 29 June 2001, 2A.

2. Ibid.

3. Donahue, "Live Your Best Life, with Oprah," 2D.

## Chapter 9 What Fills Your Tank?

1. Dr. Gary Chapman, *The Five Love Languages: How to Express Heartfelt Commitment to Your Mate* (Chicago: Northfield Publishing, 1992), 63–64.
2. Ibid., 74–75.
3. Ibid., 106.
4. Dr. Harry Schaumburg, *False Intimacy: Understanding the Struggle of Sexual Addiction* (Colorado Springs: NavPress, 1997), 175–76.

## Chapter 10 This Book Should Cost $125

1. Cathleen Fillmore, "The Houdini of Jailbirds," *The Globe and Mail,* 23 June 2001, D7.
2. For more on this, see Kevin Leman, "How to Let Your Birth Order Work for You in Business," in *The New Birth Order Book* (Grand Rapids: Revell, 1998), 190–206.

## Chapter 11 Becoming Your Own Shrink

1. This and the following accounts are taken from "The Hall of Fakes," *Sports Illustrated,* 2 July 2001, 26.
2. David Wild, "Steve Martin: The Rolling Stone Interview," *Rolling Stone,* 2 September 1999.
3. This and many other details are taken from "Steve Martin," *Current Biography,* November 2000, 385; David Wild, "Steve Martin," 88.
4. "Steve Martin," *Current Biography,* 385ff.
5. Chuck Arnold, "Chatter," *People,* 30 August 1999, 146.
6. R. J. Smith, "Steve Martin, in Revision," *The New York Times Magazine,* 8 August 1999, 28.
7. Ibid.
8. Ibid.
9. Ibid., 29.
10. Ibid.
11. Bernard Weinraub, "The Wiser Guy," *McCall's,* September 1999, 38.
12. Morris Walker, *Steve Martin: The Magic Years* (New York: S.P.I. Books, 2001), 272–73.
13. Graydon Carter, "Easy Does It," *Vanity Fair,* February 2001, 38.

For information regarding speaking engagements for businesses, churches, and civic organizations, please contact:

Dr. Kevin Leman
P.O. Box 35370
Tucson, Arizona 85740
Phone (520) 797-3830
Fax (520) 797-3809
Web site www.realfamilies.com

Others resources by Dr. Leman:

**Books:**
Adolescence Isn't Terminal—It Just Feels Like It
Becoming the Parent God Wants You to Be
Becoming a Couple of Promise
What a Difference a Daddy Makes
Making Sense of the Men in Your Life
Unlocking the Secrets of Your Childhood Memories
Living in a Stepfamily without Getting Stepped On
Bringing Up Kids without Tearing Them Down
Keeping Your Family Strong in a World Gone Wrong

**Video Series:**
Making Children Mind without Losing Yours—parenting edition
Making Children Mind without Losing Yours—public school edition for teachers, in-service sessions, PTA events
Bringing Peace and Harmony to the Blended Family
Single Parenting That WORKS!—Raising Well-Balanced Children in an Off-Balance World
Bringing Up Kids without Tearing Them Down
Keeping the Promise

Internationally known Christian psychologist, author, radio and television personality, and speaker Dr. Kevin Leman has ministered to and entertained audiences worldwide with his wit and commonsense psychology.

Best-selling author Dr. Kevin Leman has appeared on numerous radio and television programs including *Oprah, Live with Regis and Kathie Lee, The Early Show, Today, Weekend Today, CNN's American Morning with Paula Zahn, The 700 Club, Focus on the Family,* and *The View.* Dr. Leman has served as a consulting family psychologist to *Good Morning America.*

Dr. Leman is the co-founder of *realFAMILIES.com*—the television show. He is also the founder and president of Couples of Promise, an organization designed and committed to helping couples remain happily married.

Dr. Leman's twenty-one titles include the following bestsellers:

The New Birth Order Book
Making Children Mind without Losing Yours
Bringing Up Kids without Tearing Them Down
Sex Begins in the Kitchen
Say Good-bye to Stress

Sheet Music
The Perfect Match
When Your Best Is Not Good Enough
Becoming the Parent God Wants You to Be
Becoming a Couple of Promise
What a Difference a Daddy Makes
Making Sense of the Men in Your Life
Adolescence Isn't Terminal—It Just Feels Like It
Keeping Your Family Strong in a World Gone Wrong

Dr. Leman's professional affiliations include the American Psychological Association, American Federation of Radio and Television Artists, National Register of Health Services Providers in Psychology, and the North American Society of Adlerian Psychology.

Dr. Leman attended North Park College. He received his bachelor's degree in psychology from the University of Arizona, where he later earned his master's and doctorate degrees. Originally from Williamsville, New York, he and his family live in Tucson, Arizona.